CINEMAZOO
my urban safari

Library and Archives Canada Cataloguing in Publication

Oliver, Gary, 1947-
    Cinemazoo : my urban safari / Gary Oliver with Wendy Bancroft.

ISBN 978-1-8946946-2-9

1. Oliver, Gary, 1947-. 2. Cinemazoo. 3. Animal welfare—British Columbia.
4. Animal rescue—British Columbia. 5. Exotic animals—British Columbia.
6. Animals in the performing arts—British Columbia. I. Title.

HV4769 B7O43 2011   179'.309711   C2011-904601-6

Editor: Wendy Bancroft
Copy Editor: Adriana Van Leeuwen
Indexing: Renee Fossett
Cover Design: Alisha Whitley
Content Design: Omar Gallegos
Cover Photo from Gary Oliver's personal collection

All photos not credited are from Gary Oliver's private collection.

Granville Island Publishing Ltd.
212–1656 Duranleau St., Granville Island
Vancouver BC, Canada, V6H 3S4

604 688 0320
1 877 688 0320

info@granvilleislandpublishing.com
www.granvilleislandpublishing.com

First Published in 2011
Printed in Canada on recycled paper

CINEMAZOO
my urban safari

gary oliver
with wendy bancroft

GRANVILLE ISLAND
PUBLISHING

This book is dedicated to my grandfather who inspired me to go through every door that opened up to me, to my family who supported those journeys, and to my dog JAG — my best companion for 14 years. Jag was always "best in show" to me.

Contents

Prologue

Gary Oliver loves animals. He's a professional wrangler providing animals for the film industry, and he rescues exotic animals abandoned or brought to him by people who buy them and then find the animal too much to handle. With the help of a small number of staff and several volunteers, Gary cares for the animals in his refuge: Cinemazoo, located in the city of Surrey (just outside Vancouver, British Columbia). Gary started Cinemazoo over 20 years ago, and over the years the number of exotic animals in his care has risen to over 300!

Surrey and Vancouver and several other municipalities form a geographic region known as the Lower Mainland, and Gary is well known right across the region. He and his animals are frequent guests at schools, senior centres, libraries, YMCA and YWCA Kids Clubs, birthday parties, and even correctional institutes, where he enthrals audiences with the animals and spreads his message of responsible ownership and species preservation. In many ways it's the fulfilment of a dream he's had since he was a child, but it's been a rocky road to get here and that road is still full of bumps.

This is Gary's story. It's a story I first heard four years ago when Jo Blackmore, the woman who owns Granville Island Publishing, asked me to write this book. Jo was acting on behalf of a film company, which intended to produce a TV series featuring Gary and the animals and exploring the themes driving Gary's passion for animals and ecology. The book was intended to raise Gary's profile in advance of the series. However, the TV series never happened, and the book never got published because the client disappeared. The entire project got stalled.

Jo and I were both sad to see that happen. We felt Gary's life story made good reading and deserved to be told. Life went on, but the book was always a niggling thought at the back of our minds. Every so often we'd get together and say, "Hey, we really should publish that book," and then we'd get busy and the book would be put aside again.

Just before Christmas in 2009, I got a call from Gary. He and his zoo were being evicted! He hadn't been able to pay his rent and the landlord was giving him until the end of the month to find a new home for the animals and move them. Impossible, of course. It's not easy to find a home for 300 animals, and you can't move a zoo at the snap of your fingers. Fortunately, the public became aware of Gary's plight and donated enough money to pay the rent and keep the zoo going for a few months.

But then, in the spring of 2010, came another calamity. British Columbia's Department of Fish and Wildlife introduced legislation banning the importation and ownership of "dangerous" animals. The list included many of the animals Gary had rescued and that were now under his care, including his caimans and American alligators, his venomous snakes, and his snakes over three metres in length. Altogether, he had 22 animals that fell under the new Controlled Animal Species regulations. As an individual owner, rather than an accredited zoo, he would no longer be able to share these animals with the public either in a public venue or at Cinemazoo. While Gary did not take out the large American alligators nor the venomous snakes, he commonly brought caimans to presentations, as well as a lengthy boa constrictor.

In addition, animals falling under the Wildlife Act—and this included any non-domestic animals native to British Columbia—could no longer be transported without a permit. Since Gary and his crew do about 14 presentations a week and it can take weeks to get a permit, this had serious implications for Cinemazoo.

As an experienced wrangler and knowledgeable animal owner, Gary was confident in his ability to ensure there were no accidents with these animals, and felt these were the animals that made the audiences sit up and listen to what he had to say. Would he still be invited to speak if he could only bring animals commonly found in pet stores? It costs a lot to maintain the animals in the refuge, and Gary counts on the revenue from these presentations. There is more money to be made through the film industry, but those jobs are few and far between.

If he could not care for them himself, Gary was told he had nine months in which he could find new homes for the animals with accredited zoos or gain zoo accreditation himself through the Canadian Association of Zoos and Aquariums. If not, they would all be euthanized.

Thus began my renewed involvement with Gary. I'm a film-maker as well as a writer, and my background includes years as a television journalist with the Canadian Broadcasting Corporation. This story cried out to be tracked and captured. Would he be able to save the animals and save Cinemazoo? So, for the rest of 2010, I followed Gary's progress as he struggled to find some way to continue doing the work he'd spent years building. That story is documented and available online as a web series named Saving Cinemazoo.

http://www.savingcinemazoo.com

Not surprisingly, becoming immersed in this struggle provoked thoughts of the many events and adventures in Gary's life leading up to the current one and captured in the biography presented here. Jo was game and so we decided now was the time to tell the story about this fascinating character.

1 Introduction

When I was a kid, my favourite show was "Wild Kingdom," with the zoologist Marlin Perkins and his sidekick, Jim. You remember Jim. He was the guy who would actually be down in the swamp wrestling with the anaconda while Marlin sat up on a rock saying things like: "Oh, Jim's getting squeezed to death. I wonder if he's going to be able to make it?"

I didn't want to be Marlin. I wanted to be Jim, down in the swamp wrestling the snake. I was clear on which job I'd prefer but not clear at all on whether I'd ever be able to make enough money to travel to the countries where these dangerous animals lived.

Well, I did it, but instead of going to those countries, I had the alligators and snakes come to me. My wild kingdom is right here in an urban setting. I wrestle alligators regularly and I've had harrowing experiences I'll never forget. I'm living Jim's life, but I'm living it in the city.

It's weird how things turned out. Frankly, I'm not sure it would have happened if it hadn't been for my grandfather. Grandpa was a huge influence on me.

For a while, he was a millionaire—he owned a huge road construction company that paved a lot of the roads through the northern parts of Ontario. But it all ended for him, like it did for so many others, when the stock market crashed in 1929. Grandpa said that when he heard the news he just parked all his graters and machinery on the side of the road and left them. Just left them there to rust. He said there was no sense trying to keep the company going. Instead, he became a house painter. He made a decent income, but nothing like the kind of money he had before.

What really impressed me, though, was that Grandpa experienced so much in his life but was still so open to new experiences and new people.

Here's an example:

Grandpa and Grandma lived in the country, and where they lived there were hermits. I was just a kid, and to me they were pretty scary-looking characters—these people rarely ever saw baths, you know what I mean? There was this one guy, Jim Thrift. Every once in a while, Jim would come out of the bush, and when he did he'd hook up with my grandfather, who would take him into town to get stocked up on enough groceries to last for several months. Then Grandpa would bring Jim home and my grandmother would make him a good home-cooked meal.

I remember one time we were all sitting around the table—my mom, my dad, my sister, myself, my Grandpa and Grandma, and this old guy, Jim Thrift from the bush. We started to eat and the next thing you know, my mom lets out a scream. We all looked over and here Jim had taken his teeth out and put them on his plate. He said, "I'm not used to eating with these. I only wear them when I come to town, they're like dress clothes." Mom said, "Okay, but can you put a napkin over it or something?" (Of course, Jim taking his teeth out meant nothing to my grandfather).

The other thing about Grandpa was that he could tell you about something that happened in the old days and have everybody either in stitches or totally spellbound by what he was saying. And not just us kids, but the adults too. We'd all be listening to him, just fascinated by what this man was talking about.

I think what stuck with me most, though, was something he was always saying to me. "Gary," he'd say, "as you go through life, you're going to come to a lot of doors that are going to lead to a lot of different things. If the door's open, go through it. It might not always be a good experience but you're going to be learning something. You're going to have a memory from it. You may have a lot of experiences that can help you in the future, and your bad experiences can be as helpful to you as the good ones, so if the door is open: go through."

I wanted so much to be like him. I thought, "Maybe if I take these opportunities and go through these doors, someday when I'm old I'll have people around me like he did. Maybe I'll influence others like he did."

Life's pretty good right now. I've become Jim in an urban setting and, along the way, I've helped many, many people— including lots of children—get a better understanding of how precious these animals are and how they need to be protected.

So yeah, life is good, but I'm trying to stay cool about it because I've learned over the years that every time something sounded too good to be true, it *was*, and I got let down. But, you know, I've taken all the let-downs in my life pretty good and just kept moving on.

One thing I know: I've gone through a lot of doors. A lot of times it seemed like maybe I chose the wrong one and sometimes I got a bit lost, but looking back now I can see how all those experiences behind all those doors have brought me to where I am today.

2 Genesis

According to my mom, events that happened around my birth have had a lot to do with the person I've become and the life I've led.

She said that when the time came to deliver me, there was no time to get to the hospital. However, not too far from where we lived there was a huge house, and my mom had heard that it was a nurses' residence. She figured nurses were the next best thing to having a doctor, and so she told my dad to take her there. Fortunately she'd heard right, and fortunately the nurses let them in. So nurses brought me into the world, and because my mother experienced some complications after my birth, we ended up staying there for a few weeks. It was the nurses who pretty much took care of me during that time. They held me and played with me and took turns bottle-feeding me. Mom said I became their pet. She figured this was probably where I got my love of women. Well I certainly do love women—I've lived with five. Sometimes I think those nurses were just a bit too attentive.

As for my love of animals, Mom said our house overlooked a big park in Toronto and whenever we spent time in it, all the little animals would come over and visit with me. She said that must account for why I was the only one in our family that had that kind of passion for animals. She was joking, of course, but it's a good story.

My parents were middle-class; money was always a struggle. My dad was a musician and my mom worked in the art supply and stationery section of Eaton's in downtown Toronto. But we were part of a large, close-knit family and that made up for a lot. Many of my ancestors came from Italy and there was still a strong Italian influence in the family, including a musical influence. My dad played piano and so did one of his brothers and their father. One sister sang and played the accordion, and another uncle was a singer and impersonator. The only one in the whole family that didn't have any kind of a musical interest was one of the brothers, a hockey player.

The parties were fantastic. There was always lots of music, dancing and singing, and other kinds of entertainment.

I'll never forget this one skit my uncle and dad used to do. My dad would be on the piano playing, and my uncle would sit down beside him and start to play the bass part of the song—my dad would be playing the other keys—and they'd start to play a duet together. Then, all of a sudden, my dad would look over to my uncle and say, "You just hit one of my notes!" My uncle would say, "No, I didn't." And they'd keep this up while they continued to play the piece.

"Yeah, you did, I saw ya'."

"No, I didn't."

"Oh, okay . . . wait a minute, you just did it again!"

"I did not!"

So then my dad would hit one of my uncle's notes. And they always had this mafia look, you know? The way they looked at one another, it was gangster-like.

They'd start hitting one another's notes real hard, but they wouldn't lose the tune at all. By the end of the song, they were wrestling on the floor. It was so funny.

My dad couldn't read a note of music yet he was always in demand: never without a job: played for the biggest companies; played for banquets, and things like that. Later he played in clubs. The downside of my dad being a musician was that I didn't get a lot of time with him. He'd go to work in the evening and wouldn't come home until the wee hours. And of course he slept during the day, so he'd be sleeping when I was around. I spent more time with my mom, but she wasn't a really outwardly affectionate person. I can remember one time when I was a kid and I was going to camp. Instead of giving me a hug, she shook my hand and said,

"Have a good time." I mean, I'm laughing now, but at the time it kind of felt like a business deal.

Anyway, the thing is that my parents didn't have a lot of money, and like lots of people without money, we moved a lot.

I remember one place we lived in when I was about five or six years old, above a grocery store at one end of the block. Across the street on the other corner was this older lady, and she had a really nice house with a beautiful garden. My sister and I used to go over there and play in her backyard and she had these big cement lions in her garden. Apparently I was always on those lions. I would sit on them and I'd sleep in between their paws and she'd come out and find me there. She said that I was obsessed with them. I guess that was really the first little hint about how much I loved animals; that, and the fact that I was always looking in the garden for bugs.

But overall, until the age of six, I was just a normal kid growing up. Then I came down with rheumatic fever and my life totally changed.

3 On Golden Ponds

It hit me hard. Rheumatic fever was very serious in those days. I guess they didn't have the treatments that they have for it today. Anyway, I was bedridden for a year.

I would get these high fevers—a couple of times they had to rush me to the hospital because I got so dehydrated. The fevers got so bad they affected the nerves in my legs, and I became paralyzed for about five or six months. Mom had to carry me everywhere, and with my body so weak, my resistance was low and so I seemed to catch every other illness around me (jaundice, measles, mumps, tonsillitis). It all hit me at once.

Then there were all the needles. Every few days for that entire year the doctor would come and take blood to test. I hated the needles.

All of that took its toll. By the time I was strong enough to get out of bed, I'd missed a year of school. I'd had some tutoring, but it didn't help. I think I was probably too sick to comprehend what was going on. Also, although I was able to walk, I was still very weak, especially in my legs. I couldn't skate, I couldn't swim, I couldn't run, I couldn't bicycle; I just didn't have the strength. All my friends were doing this kind of stuff and I always felt left out.

Right about this time, we went to stay with my Uncle Ted and Aunt Marie for a while. Mom had taken the year off work to take care of me, and by the end of that year my parents were really broke. My aunt and uncle were rich. They had a house in Rosedale—one of the wealthiest areas in Toronto—and a beautiful cottage at Lake Simcoe, where we used to visit them for holidays. They offered to take us in until Mom and Dad got back on their feet. I was pretty happy about that. For one thing, it meant lots of time up at the cottage. I loved being up there, and my uncle, Ted Davy, was kind of amazing.

He made his first fortune after the war by buying and fixing up used cars and selling them for big money. At one point, he had the largest used car lot in Toronto. I'd hear jingles on the radio advertising his car lot and go "Hey, that's my uncle!" It was neat. From used cars, he went into property development and bought up some gambling casinos in Nevada. He got to know a lot of famous people in Nevada, some of whom I met on my visits to the cottage. You see, my uncle had several planes—seaplanes—that he would dock at the edge of the lake. He'd pick these guys up in Nevada and bring them back to the cottage. They'd all go on fishing trips and things like that.

One of the famous people who came up was John Wayne. I'm told he used to pick me up and put me over his head onto his shoulders, and there I'd be, riding around on John Wayne's shoulders! To me, he was just a big guy like my uncle, who was six foot–five. I met other famous people too, like Johnny Weiss- muller (one of the first actors to play Tarzan) and Whipper Billy Watson (a big-time wrestler). He and my uncle used to spend a lot of time together. I mean, I didn't actually know who they were at the time—I was too young—but my parents told me when I was a bit older, and I went "Wow, you're kidding? You mean HE carried me on his back?"

Anyway, I had some pretty good times at that cottage. A few pretty scary times, too. I remember one time when we had a huge lightning storm and I got left outside. Not intentionally, of course. We'd all been having breakfast on their screened-in patio. It was nice on that patio: looking out from it, you had a decent view of Lake Simcoe. So we were sitting there one morning and we could see this storm coming across the lake—a big black cloud. I remember thinking it was the coolest thing, that you could actually watch the storm come.

Finally it hit. It rained and hailed; there was thunder and light- ning. We weren't worried. We had the screened-in patio, so we just continued sitting there and eating breakfast. All of a sudden a great big bolt of lightning came down and split a tree in half about 25 feet away from the house. The force shook everything off the table. Of course we all jumped up and ran to get inside the house.

I was the closest to the door, but when I jumped up, I fell. Everyone was panicking and didn't notice me; in fact, they ran over top of me. My mother, who thought I was already in the house, ran in and slammed the door . . . on my fingers, because I was still trying to get in. So I'm out there screaming my lungs out because my fingers were being squashed. Finally, they heard me and opened the door, grabbed my arm and pulled me in. My mom felt pretty terrible.

Another time—before that, when I was only about five years old—I went outside and sat on a wasp nest on a little mound by a tree; the same tree that got struck by lightning. Kind of an unlucky tree, now that I think of it. Anyway, apparently the wasps came swarming out of the nest and my mom and aunt heard me screaming, so they came running out of the house to see what was going on. Well, all those wasps were just going at me. I had shorts on and they were all over my legs and some were on my neck. My legs puffed up. Mom had to take me to the hospital to get some antivenom.

But mostly it was good times, so when my aunt and uncle invited us up there after this really hard year we'd had with me with rheumatic fever and all, I didn't mind going there at all. I had fun, too, except I was still pretty weak so I couldn't do things like swim when we went to the beach. Instead, while the others were swimming, I'd sit on the dock and fish and try to catch pollywogs and frogs and things like that.

One day this boy came over to the cottage to visit. He was only two years older than me so I'm pretty sure my aunt asked him over to keep me company. My aunt told me his name was Eugene McSweeney. I've never forgotten that name (and wherever you are today, Eugene, thanks). My aunt said, "Eugene collects insects."

"Oh, really?" I said.

"Yeah," she said. "Maybe he'd take you on a field trip."

So she asked him, and he said, "Yeah, sure. Come on along."

Eugene took me on this field trip and showed me insects in the bushes, in the fields, under trees. I remember he showed me a big cocoon that I would have missed entirely if he hadn't been there. I would have just walked right by it thinking it was just a dry leaf. He showed me praying mantises and all kinds of things. I was constantly saying things like "Wow, this is so cool. I didn't know we had all these."

Then Eugene took me back to his parents' cottage, where he had insects mounted in cigar boxes. He had about 20 boxes of insects. I kept opening lids and seeing more and more amazing insects. I'd ask him, "Where did you get this one? What country is this from?" and he would say, "That's from here." I'd say, "No way!" I couldn't believe that all these beautiful animals were right in my backyard.

That's when the bug bit me, so to speak. I knew I wanted to collect insects and I knew this was something I was strong enough to do. Eugene taught me a bit about collecting to get me started, and that was it. There was no looking back.

4 Bugs in the Bedroom

I became obsessed by anything to do with animals. I couldn't get enough. That was when I started watching "Wild Kingdom." I also began to collect all kinds of bugs and kept them in my room.

One thing I give my parents a lot of credit for is the degree to which they tolerated my obsession. I mean, my dad hated spiders and my mom really hated snakes, and I tortured her with them whenever I found them. Up at the cottage I'd come walking up with six snakes in each hand and say, "Look what I found!" She'd be running down the field as fast as she could, screaming, "Get rid of those things!"

My sister has a phobia of snakes to this day because I threw one at her when I was about eight years old. She was six at the time. We were at my grandfather's house and she was on a swing. I found a dead snake and started swinging it in the air, just pretending I was going to throw it at her. She was yelling, "Get away from me!" and then all of a sudden the tail broke off the snake—I mean, the snake was dead and rotting—and as it did, she was coming up on the swing so it wrapped right around her leg.

Well, she screamed, came flying off the swing, and went running down the track toward my Grandpa's house, shaking her leg and screaming and trying to get the thing off of her.

She went into the house and I knew, right then and there,

that I was in trouble. So I casually walked down the lane, into the house, and right past everybody—they were just looking at me wondering what I was doing—and went straight upstairs to my room. There was a hole in the floor with a plate over it that used to be for a stovepipe. I lifted up the plate and looked down into the living room and asked, "How long do I have to stay up here?" (Because my punishment was always to go and stay in my room, and I knew I was going to be punished).

But they never suppressed my obsession. They supported it by buying me books and microscopes—anything to do with animals. I guess they kept thinking it was a fad, that I'd grow out of it, but I didn't. I just kept getting more and more and more interested. I had all this stuff in my bedroom—all my animals, my microscopes and everything. My bedroom was on the second floor of the house. It was an old kitchen so there were lots of cupboards and I had a sink for my aquariums. It was really perfect for me.

I loved bugs. Bugs and art . . . well, drawings of bugs. If you read my report cards from when I was a kid you'll see that I excelled in science and art, but everything else was a struggle for me. It's funny. The other day I was going through some photos and I came across this brown wrinkled-up piece of paper that was falling apart. I opened it gently and found that it was a picture of a puppy dog with his paw up, done in pencil. There was a ribbon on it. I had won first place for an art competition when I was 11 years old at a club called the Dovercourt Boys' Club.

My mom always said I was good at doodling. I was always drawing animals. She encouraged it because she painted and drew pictures herself. So did my Mom's sister, my wealthy aunt. My aunt actually had a big art studio in her house. They both encouraged me to go for the arts. The teacher used to say "If Gary could put as much attention into his other studies as he does art and science, he'd be an honour student. But he has far too much to say to the students around him." I was always showing the other kids my bugs. Looking back I know that my bug show-and-tells were a way for me to make friends. I was behind in a lot of ways having missed that year of school, including socially. Having the bugs gave me a bit of status with the other kids.

I was always on the lookout for insects, no matter where I was. I was always collecting them and bringing them home. This sometimes got me into trouble . . . like that one time when I was around 11 and we were staying at my Grandpa's place, when I collected the butterfly chrysalides.

There was this big field there full of milkweed plants. Now, milkweed plants are natural feeding plants for caterpillars, and I swear every plant in this field had these caterpillars on it. I could see there were two species—the ones I recognized were Monarchs, while the others (I later learned) were Mourning Cloaks.

I could also see that many of them were going into the pupation, or "chrysalides" stage. I started gathering them all up. I collected several hundred of them and brought them back to my home in Toronto and put them in my bedroom. I had them in boxes, Petri dishes—I had them everywhere. My parents, of course, had no idea I'd done this.

One day I came home from school and my mom said, "We have a problem." I said, "What problem?" I was thinking maybe an animal had gotten loose or something. She said, "Come up to your room with me." I said, "Okay."

So up to the room we went and she opened up the door and it was like, psychedelic. It had been a really hot day that day and I guess that triggered it, you know? All the chrysalides had turned into butterflies. When butterflies first emerge, they pump their wings to get the blood into them, so all these butterflies were pumping their wings. It was like neon signs flashing all over the place. All the walls, my bedspread and pillow, the cupboards, the drapes, everything was just covered in bright orange Monarchs and Mourning Cloaks with their iridescent blackish-purple wings and yellow trim.

I was just standing there going, "Wow! This is so cool!" A bit sarcastically, Mom said, "Yeah, real cool," but then admitted that it was actually really pretty.

We stood there looking at the scene for a while, and then she said, "What are you going to do with them all?" I said, "I don't know yet."

Then she asked, "Where are you going to sleep?"

"Can I sleep on the couch tonight?"

"Okay, but you've got to get rid of them. You're not going to be sleeping on the couch until they die of old age, you know."

"No, I'll find a way tonight. I'll think of something."

Then she said, "Why don't you let them go?"

I said, "Well, yeah, I'm going to keep a few and I'll let the rest go."

Then a light came on. I thought, "Why not make a thing out of it?"

I went around the whole neighbourhood and told kids there was going to be this big nature show in my backyard. I told them if they wanted to come, they'd have to pay a fee; I think it was a dime. About 15 kids showed up. They all paid their dime and came over to my backyard.

They said, "I don't see anything." I said, "No, no. Sit down on the grass; the show is about to begin." So they all got themselves a spot on the backyard grass and I said, "I'll be doing the show from my bedroom window, up top there."

"Okay," they said.

So I went upstairs, got a broom, opened up the window and started brushing the butterflies toward it. All those hundreds of butterflies went flying out the window with their different colours. The kids loved it. They were all going "Oooh! Aaaaaah! Wow!" They were amazed that I had had all those butterflies in my bedroom.

Eventually, though, it got to the point where my parents began getting a little nervous about all those animals. Finally they said, "You can have the whole basement. It can be your little zoo down there. But if anything whatsoever crawls over the top step of that basement that isn't human, you're going to die the youngest kid on the street. If I find a spider or a snake, you're history!" Believe me, I kept a good eye on my animals to make sure that didn't happen.

***

When I was 12 years old, I started volunteering at the Royal Ontario Museum. I used to go to the museum frequently because they had these cases where you could see beautiful insects from all over the world.

One day I went by one of the doors inside the museum and noticed that it said "Entomology Department" on it. By then I'd read enough about insects to know what entomology meant, so I knocked on it and walked in. There were several scientists there. They asked me what I wanted, so I told them how interested I was in insects. One of the professors said "Oh, I've seen you in the museum several times." I said, "Yeah, I keep coming to look in the bug cases." He said, "Yes, well, it's pretty clear you do have a love for them." Then he said, "Well, if you want to come around, maybe we can give you some chores to do." You know, it was kind of like being in a Harry Potter book.

In the beginning I only got to do things like wash the slides and clean the floor, but they began to make the responsibilities more and more interesting. I started labelling insects, and after they saw some of my doodles, they realized I had artistic talent and started getting me to do illustrations for some of their lectures. I even did some sketches for their books. I've still got some of those drawings today (they're just rough sketches, mind you).

As I got a little older, around 14 or 15, I became more serious about collecting. However, my interest also shifted to collecting species from outside of Canada.

I started to approach anyone I knew who would be travelling overseas. I knew it wouldn't be my own family—we never went any further than to my aunt and uncle's cottage at Lake Simcoe, or to my grandfather's home in Bracebridge. That was all my parents could afford. But my aunt travelled, and sometimes other people I met did as well.

I'd beg them to find a science shop or a museum wherever they were, and try to get the names of anybody who had anything to do with animals, especially insects. Then I'd correspond with that person and ask them if they could set me up with an amateur insect collector. If they were able to do this, I'd write and establish a rapport with that collector.

At that time, I knew a little more about rearing large moths like Lunas and Cecropias. I learned how to raise them and I bred several generations. I would mount them and send them off to fellow collectors overseas, and they would send me boxed insects from their countries.

We'd be getting these boxes in the mail on a regular basis, so my parents decided to build a big wooden chest-type box with a lock and key that sat on the veranda of our house. The postman had a key to the box, so whenever he came with an insect delivery, he'd just put the box in there because nothing fit through the mail slot anymore.

I never knew what I was getting. I'd open up the box and there'd be these giant stag beetles from South America. One time I opened up a box and it had three scorpions in it . . . and they were still alive! I guess there were no customs rules or regulations about this stuff in those days.

By the time I was around 18 years old, I had 10,000 specimens in my collection. By the time I was 19, I was elected the first president of the Toronto chapter of the Michigan Entomology Society. However, I stepped down from that after the first year because, although I knew a lot about insects for my age, I didn't feel that I could match some of the professors at the university, nor some of the entomologists that had joined the club.

So why didn't I take up entomology as a formal study? Well, the professors at the museum were encouraging me to pursue that kind of academic route, but like I said, I was a pretty lousy student except for art and science. I did want to be a vet, but my parents just didn't have the money to fund that kind of schooling. They could barely feed us and house us and get us through regular school, let alone vet school. I tried to do it on my own, working part-time, but I was too tired to keep up my studies.

I always got hand-me-downs. My rich aunt had a son, Doug. Everything I wore was a hand-me-down from Doug. I used to have identity confusion and think I was Doug because everything I wore was monogrammed with his name. All my toys were from him, too. Everything. My parents did the best they could: they bought us stuff, but if the kids in the neighbourhood got bicycles, I got one a year or two later.

It didn't bother me, though, you know. It really didn't. Because I had my animals. Maybe I couldn't be a vet, but I knew I would do something with animals. (Or I would be an artist, one or the other). But animals opened up worlds to me that nothing else could have. You know?

To see Gary with his insects,. watch this episode from the web series:

http://www.savingcinemazoo.com/episode4.html

5 Spreading my Own Wings

I kept on loving animals and bugs and kept on collecting but by the time I turned 13, I was starting to get stronger and was anxious to be more physical. I wanted to do some of the things the other guys were doing (well, that they *had* been doing). Typical of my development in those days: just when all my friends were beginning to get out of sports, I was getting into them.

I decided I wanted to play hockey. I wanted to be a goalie because I wouldn't have to skate that much. Fortunately, the team I joined needed a goalie, so I was set.

Our games all took place at the George Bell Arena, located just a few blocks from the Swift Premium packers' slaughterhouse. We'd always walk by the place when we were heading to and from the games, and before long, the slaughterhouse became more of a focus for me than playing hockey. There were, after all, animals in the slaughterhouse.

There were bulls—well, actually, they were steers—and they were all out in the open in pens. I couldn't resist climbing over the fence to get to the railings of the pens that held the animals. Then I could reach through and pat them and play with them.

One day this kid I was with said, "Hey, you ever thought of getting on one of those things?" I said "No." He said, "Well, we've got all our equipment on. How can we get hurt?" "Oh," I said, "that's true. Okay." I always liked watching bull-riding.

So every week after our hockey game was over, we'd go and try to ride the steers. It's amazing we didn't get killed. One time I got tossed two pens over from where I'd started. I'd fall and be under their feet and they'd be trampling and all freaked out. This other guy and I would just be killing ourselves laughing. I figured I had all my hockey shins on, elbow pads and helmet and everything, so I couldn't get hurt. I was nervous, yeah, but I was a kid. You think you're invincible, right?

We did that until one day when we got caught and received a stiff warning about not coming onto the property. It was fun while it lasted, although part of me felt bad about tormenting these poor animals that were about to get slaughtered. Then again, maybe it was the last bit of fun they had.

Not long after that, my parents split up and I moved with my mother and sister to stay with my aunt in Etobicoke, a city just outside Toronto. This put an end to my bull-riding goalie days and opened up a whole new chapter in my life.

6 Lonnie Tunes

We had actually stayed with my aunt and uncle once before, when I was seven and they'd been living in Rosedale, a wealthy suburb of Toronto. It was the year I was sick and Mom had quit her job to take care of me. By the end of that year, family finances were pretty dim, so my aunt offered to take us in. We only stayed for six months before moving back into a house of our own but unfortunately, things were still hard for us financially. My parents were broke all the time and eventually, things between them broke too. When I was 13, they decided to separate. By then, my aunt and uncle had split up as well and my aunt had moved to Etobicoke and was living in a big house there. My mom, my sister, and I moved in with her.

I wasn't happy about my parents splitting up and I missed my neighbourhood and friends in Toronto, but moving to Etobicoke meant meeting and becoming friends with Lonnie, and that made up for lots.

Lonnie lived across the street. He had a huge house and I would see him out playing in the front lawn all the time. Finally I went over and met him. We became best friends; we just clicked.

Lonnie was so much fun. He wanted to try everything and I was right there with him. For instance, lots of kids walk on stilts, but we didn't just walk on regular stilts: we tried to make the stilts as high as we could. We built them so high we were eventually walking on stilts where the only way we could get on them was from the roof of a house. We knew it was dangerous but we'd get on and see how far we could walk down the front lawn before we'd crash.

We made tonnes of stuff: sail-carts and go-karts, pool tables and trampolines. It was always something. We made a pole vault in the field next to where we lived and then got into pole-vaulting in a serious way. We joined a gymnastics club when I was about 14, and I got really good at the parallel bars. I won all the competitions at school. It was good for me, and I gained back a lot of the strength I'd lost in my earlier years.

We made a list of things to do because we never wanted to be bored, and we kept adding to it. Lonnie's dad owned a bakery that had a big industrial dryer, and more than once we took turns dressing up in this big raccoon fur coat and riding around the dryer. We were smart enough to wear a helmet and make sure the door was open and the air wasn't on super hot, but it was still a crazy thing to do.

One of the things on our list was taking people on hikes through the sewers.

We'd found an entrance way to a sewer system through some bent bars and we would go through them and into the system and hike for miles. We learned all the routes through all the passage-ways. Not content with amusing ourselves, we decided to start a business charging kids for taking them through the sewers. We called them "Sewer Tours."

We'd get about six kids and head off through the system until we came to this one big huge section where all the sewers came together. That's where we'd stop and have lunch.

One time we came to this spot and we actually met up with a bunch of other kids we knew who had come out through another system. So we all hung out there together, had a great time. When it was time to head back, we decided we didn't want to walk all the way back because we were tired. I mean, you had to walk all hunched over, right? Lonnie and I had scars on our backs from hitting the ceilings of the sewers. Anyway, we decided to come up a manhole. The trick was finding the right manhole—we always had to push the lid up a bit and peek out to see if the coast was clear. We came to this one manhole and peeked out and we could see grass around it so we knew we weren't in the middle of a road. I could hear a loud motor running but I couldn't see anything so I said, "This looks like a safe place. Let's all get out here." I flipped the lid over and was just starting to climb out when I felt somebody grab the back of my neck and yank me right up. This guy pulled me out and yelled down, "The rest of you kids come on out."

Turns out the motor I heard was this guy cutting his lawn. The sewer ran right along the edge of his lawn. It took a long time for everyone to climb out, because including the other guys we'd met, there were about 15 of us. He gave us a real good lecture and warned us that if we ever did that again, we'd be going to jail. He was trying to scare us, and it worked: we were scared. However, that didn't stop us from going through the sewers. We kept doing that until the city found the bent bars and blocked up that entrance.

Lonnie and I got into so much trouble. I mean, I was capable of pulling pranks on my own, but Lonnie really accentuated that part of me. I'd say the only way in which I was more daring than Lonnie was in meeting girls.

I always loved girls. Maybe it was those nurses when I was born, but whatever it was, right from day one of public school I was interested in girls. Lonnie was totally the opposite. He was really awkward around them.

I was always trying to fix him up, but it never seemed to work. Like, we'd be going to do something, like going to the skating rink, and I'd say, "Okay, Lonnie, I've got this girl lined up for you, she's a real sweetheart and she's a friend of my girlfriend so we can like, double-date, okay?"

Well, we'd all get to the rink and he'd get on the ice and go zoom-zoom-zooming around like he was a speed skater. The girl would go, "Where is he?" And we wouldn't see Lonnie again. I'd end up with both the girls on my arms, which was okay.

One time he and I were in the hydro field and I found a brown paper bag. I kicked it and it tinkled, so I opened it up and found it was full of these pewter rings with little hearts on them that we used to give to a girl if you wanted to go steady. There were a lot of them, so I gave seven of them away to seven different girls. I never told any one of them about the others. I was basically going steady with seven girls at one time. In my mind, I was just getting rid of the rings and having fun. But then I met a girl I really liked and I said to Lonnie, "I've got to get rid of these other girls because I'm getting myself in a mess here."

So I told each girl I had something really important to talk to her about and asked them to meet me at this one restaurant where we all hung out. I told them to arrive at a particular time and to sit in a particular booth—this one that was shaped like a horseshoe. I staggered all the times for them to arrive five minutes apart, and I told them it was really important to come precisely at that time. And I asked Lonnie and a couple of other buddies to sit in the next booth so they could hear what was going on and report back to me. I, of course, would not be there. It didn't take long before they were asking each other:

"Oh what are you doing here?"

"Well, I'm meeting Gary."

"Well, so am I"

"So am I."

"What're you meeting Gary for?"

"Well, he's my boyfriend."

"He's my boyfriend!"

And they all had the same ring on, you know? I realize now it was a bit cruel but I thought it was hilarious at the time.

Lonnie came back and he said, "If I were you, I'd change schools because you're going to get lynched." Oh, they were livid. They were just livid, and they were planning all these nasty things to do to me. Ultimately they decided not to speak to me. Not one word. They'd pass me by, and I'd say, "Hi," and they wouldn't talk to me. And they didn't for a long time. But that's okay, because I'd found a new girl to go out with.

In all other ways, though, Lonnie was the leader.

***

We stayed with my aunt until I was 15, then Mom moved into an apartment in Toronto, so my sister and I moved in with her there. She and my dad still weren't speaking and she was going out with this guy I didn't like. I wanted my dad back—and I managed to get him back—but I've always wondered if it was the right thing to do.

Basically, I lied to them.

Dad used to play piano for the Eaton's Christmas banquets. Mom was back working at Eaton's and the event was coming up. They wanted my dad to play again, so they asked her to arrange it. Of course Mom wasn't talking to my dad, so she called me and said, "Gary, can you ask your father if he would play for the banquet this year. Tell him I won't be there." I phoned my dad and delivered the message: "Mom wants you to play and she said she wouldn't be there." He said, "Okay, if she's not going to be there, I'll do the job."

But then I phoned the boss and told him that my dad would do the job only if the boss would tell my mom that my dad would *not* be doing the job. He agreed. I figured then Mom would go to the banquet and that if they showed up together, they'd start talking again and, if they started talking again, they might see things differently.

Sure enough, this is exactly what happened and they did get back together. But you know, from that point on they seemed to vegetate. They got along okay but they never did anything together, and that became a big bone of contention between my dad and me because he was the one with the wheels. My mom didn't drive. I'd always say, "Well, why don't you and Mom go out to a play, or go to a movie? There're some really good movies on now. Or go to bingo? Do something."

"Ah, no, we're fine. Your mom doesn't want to do that."

I'd say, "How do you know she doesn't want to do that?" and, "You're just sitting here, day in, day out. You work, you come home, you eat, you drink your bottle of wine and you go to sleep. You get up and do the same thing every day. Nothing changes. You're wasting your life."

Because me, I'm all for *doing*, you know? I mean, I'll go to a trade show on quilting because I don't know anything about quilting and I figure I might learn something or meet some cool people or whatever. Just because I've never done it before. But I couldn't get them to see that. They just existed together. They did their job, went home, slept, ate, and that was it.

Fortunately I wasn't with them through this period. Mom had been living in a one-bedroom apartment and I'd been sleeping on the couch, but once Dad moved back in, the place got too crowded. So when my aunt invited me to move back, my parents said okay.

Etobicoke is only eleven kilometres southwest of Toronto so it wasn't like I was moving a long distance away. In fact, I'd kept seeing Lonnie and my other friends in Etobicoke when I'd been living with my mom in Toronto. All in all, it felt great to be back and this time I was a bit older. The adventures with Lonnie escalated.

Animals were still a big part of my life and I continued to enjoy drawing and painting, but Lonnie opened up the "do crazy things" door to being a normal teenager—the mischievous part. We were both up for trying different things and had no interest in doing stuff like hanging around in malls. When I think about some of the things we did, it was a little crazier than the usual teenage stuff, but I felt that it was okay for me to experience that and I wanted to do it. We had a lot of fun, and for the most part we managed to stay out of trouble.

7 Behind
the Crazy Things Door

Like I said, Lonnie's dad owned a big bakery in Toronto, and from the time we were about 14 or so, Lonnie and I earned extra money working in it.

One of our jobs was to service the 52 bakery trucks, and because it had to be done on a day there were no deliveries, it meant that every Sunday after church we'd head straight to the bakery garage. One of the guys would bring the trucks over from the bakery, three blocks away, and then Lonnie and I would fill up the gas, check the oil, check the water in the radiator and the battery, and then he'd drive it back. Eventually we started driving them back and forth between the bakery and the garage— the guy didn't say anything about it—and that's how I learned how to drive.

Lonnie's dad treated me like I was his own son because I hung around so much. He'd say, "You're gonna hang around my son, you're gonna live in my house, you're gonna take the same punishment that my kids do." Sunday mornings were especially tense because his dad would always make us get up and go to church before we had to head to the bakery, and getting up was the last thing we wanted to do. It usually followed a pattern. First Lonnie's dad would yell out; "Come on boys, get up!" We'd ignore him. He'd do it a couple more times, and then he'd come down and pull the blankets off of us—we slept in this great big king-sized bed. If we didn't get up then, he'd walk out of the room and come back with a bucket of ice water that he'd throw on us. That usually worked.

I remember one Sunday morning, however, when we'd been up all night partying and there was no way we wanted to get up and go to church and then work. Lonnie decided we weren't. He said, "No matter what dad does, don't get up. We're not getting up." I said, "Okay."

Sure enough, Lonnie's dad yelled for us to get up, and then when we didn't, he pulled the blankets off of us. He got a bucket of ice water and threw that over us. Lonnie knew exactly what he was going to do each time. He said, "No matter what, we're not getting up." So, we lay there in the soaking wet bed, pulled the blanket back off the floor and covered ourselves up again.

Then he left us alone for a little bit and I thought maybe he'd given up. I was just drifting back to sleep when all of a sudden my foot was grabbed from below. Lonnie's dad had snuck in the room and grabbed our feet, which were sticking out of the bed, with a pair of pliers! He was holding on to our toes and I said, "I'm up, I'm up, I'm getting up!" I said, "Lonnie, I can't take it!"

The ironic thing is that his dad always told me I was the one influencing his son. This was definitely not the case. Lonnie was the leader. I can't remember ever saying anything but "okay" when Lonnie suggested we do something crazy.

One evening Lonnie and I were all alone in the bakery when we got the bright idea to jump in the dough vats. "Okay." These were metal vats ten feet long and three feet deep that held the mounds of dough made in the mixing machines. The mixers were also huge—you had to go up a ladder to get on top of them to clean them. Once the vats were filled with dough from the mixing machines, they'd be rolled into a cooling room to keep until the bakers came in the next day to pull out the dough and make the bread and other baking goods.

Anyway, we pulled one of the vats out of the cooling room, climbed up the ladder, took off our clothes, and dove into the dough that, of course, stuck to us. We kept on doing this until we were completely covered with dough except for our eyes and then we went outside and scared a bunch of little kids. After that bit of fun we came back in, scraped the dough off and put it back in the vats, patted it down, and then rolled the vat back in to the cooling room. Next day, they made bread out of that dough.

Let's see, what else? Oh, yeah. When we'd work in the bakery on our summer holidays, we'd pack Kaiser rolls into bags, give the bag a twist, put it through a machine, and put the bag in a box. For fun, though, we'd sometimes get the bun just when it came out of the oven and the bread dough in the middle was soft, and we'd pull the dough out and roll it into a ball. Those dough balls would bounce just like a rubber ball. We'd get about 20 of those each and then on our breaks we would have Kaiser roll ball fights, running around the bakery.

One of the other things we'd do is take all the baking leftovers that had been stored in the cupboards at the bakery and sell them around the neighbourhood. We used to get our gas money that way.

Lonnie and I started getting into cars. Having his dad own a garage was a real plus for us because it gave us a place we could work on them. We customized a '55 Chevy and we built a stock car. I was really into cars at that time. Probably the animals took a back seat for a little while in that period of my life because I really enjoyed fixing up those cars.

It was great. The hangout during the summer was a place called Wasaga Beach and we could always go there on the weekends because we had our own car. On top of that, we were getting our gas free from the bakery trucks. What we'd do was, when we were filling the trucks with gas, we'd mark down that we put 12 gallons in but we'd really only put 10. We had this great big oil tank that we would fill up with gas and we'd keep it for ourselves for our summer adventures. I know we were bad, but Lonnie's dad had lots of money and he underpaid us.

Of course we never paid to get into anything. We'd do things like walk backwards into a building as if we were leaving. We found a way to get into the grandstand at the exhibition grounds by taking a service elevator to the roof and then taking some stairs down to the grandstand. Or, we'd risk getting killed in traffic by running across the expressway by the exhibition grounds so that we could jump the fence into the grounds. We'd get chased by security guards, so we'd split up and then arrange to meet at a certain point once we lost the people chasing us. It was always an adventure, you know?

Speaking of getting chased, one of the things Lonnie and I used to do was to sneak in to the neighbours' pools after midnight when everyone was asleep and go skinny-dipping. One night we decided to try out a pool we'd seen at a big house across the ravine from where Lonnie lived. There was a creek in the ravine and we had to cross the creek and go through a field to get to the house which was up on the hill on the other side. It was a huge pool located quite a distance away from the house and it was one-thirty in the morning and no one was around so we figured we were safe. We stripped off our clothes and jumped in.

All of a sudden we heard dogs and then we saw these two huge Great Danes coming down from the house. So we jumped out of the pool and we started running through the hedges and down into the ravine. Those dogs chased us until we got to the other side of the creek, and even then we didn't stop running. We ran up the hill on our side and back into Lonnie's house. But we had no clothes on, we didn't even have time to get our towels or anything, so we were butt-naked and also ripped to shreds from the thorn bushes that we'd been running through. We spent the rest of the night trying to pull out the thorns and sop up the blood from the scratches.

That sort of ended the skinny-dipping days, but you know, those days . . . it was like, if anybody said, "Let's try this," or "Let's do this," as long there wasn't a risk of getting caught or breaking the law to any degree of seriousness, I thought, "Yeah, okay. Why not?"

I remember one time we were sitting in a restaurant at Wasaga Beach and the people sitting behind us were talking about this beautiful cottage right on the beach that was for sale. One of them said, "Yeah, that cottage is for sale every summer. I wonder why nobody buys it?" And we heard the other person say, "Well, because all they do is put a for-sale sign on it with a number for the realtor, they don't really try to sell it. The people who own it use it every winter when they come up for skiing on Blue Mountain, and then close it down when they go to Europe in the summer."

So Lonnie and I got talking and decided to go and check the place out.

We found a way to get into the cottage. Well, okay, we broke in. We took notepads with us and we diagrammed exactly how everything was. We drew exactly where the coffee table was, and noted the ashtray was there, and this little ornament was there and so on. We did this throughout the whole house. Then we took down the "For Sale," sign, and once we got the front door unlocked from the inside, it became our cottage for three years in a row. We'd go up and spend the whole summer there, and we had a great time.

We'd invite our friends and tell girls that we were orphans and that this was part of what our parents left us when they died—they left us the cottage along with the house in Etobicoke and the car and everything else like that. Like we were on our own at 16 or 17 years old—that's all we were. And these girls would feel sorry for us. It was a lot of fun. Then we'd put it all back together exactly as it was when we'd leave at the end of the summer.

I wasn't a drinker, though. The only time I did that was on a New Year's Eve when I was 16.

Lonnie's parents were in Florida so we had the house to ourselves. In the past, we'd "borrowed" a couple of bottles of Black Velvet whisky from his sister's wedding and we'd hidden them in the attic, thinking maybe we'd drink them one day when we had a celebration about something. Well, New Year's came along and we felt it was a good enough reason to celebrate, so we brought those two 26-ounce bottles of Black Velvet whisky down and proceeded to drink. We had no mix and I'd never had whiskey before in my life. It was hard getting it down, but we'd kind of challenged ourselves to do it. You know, "How much can you drink?"

We consumed an awful lot that day. And then we also had these pizzas that his dad made in the bakery. We drank all that whisky and we ate a lot of pizza. Oh boy, I'll tell you, before midnight we were starting to feel real sick. I remember I couldn't hold it back anymore and I ran into the bathroom and started spewing into the toilet. Lonnie came in and saw me and that made him sick he started spewing too. So we were both standing there spewing into the toilet . . . only the seat was closed so it was going all over the floor.

When we got up in the morning, we saw that somehow, the fish tank had broken. I can't remember how, I only know the aftermath of that night. So the fish tank was broken, and they had shag carpets in those days, so there were guppies and angelfish and everything stuck in it. Oh, yeah, and the canary was dead. We don't know what happened to the canary. There was taffy everywhere. I vaguely recall Lonnie saying at some point in the evening that he knew how to make taffy so we'd tried cooking some. Well, it was on the floor, it was on the counters, it was on the cupboards, and it was stuck in the carpet—it was everywhere. And also, there was a big mirror broken in this cabinet his mother had.

We had approximately a week to straighten the place out before they returned from Florida. We did it. It was kind of weird going around to pet stores with a dead canary, trying to find a similar one, because it had little markings on its wings that we needed to match. We finally found one that looked almost identical and brought it home and put it in the cage. We fixed the mirror; we got everything cleaned up. We took the fish tank right out and told his parents when they came back that we didn't want it anymore, so we'd given it to some friends of ours.

Things started to get funny at the breakfast table about a week after they came back. Lonnie's mother said to his father, "You know, Walter, I'm sure Joey's happy we're back from Florida." Joey was the canary. Lonnie's dad said, "Why do you say that?" "Well, it never used to sing this much." Lonnie and I were trying to hold it back and not look at each other.

The very next day, we're at breakfast again and Lonnie's dad says to his mother, "Molly, while I'm at work today, phone the furnace people and tell them to come in and check the furnace, will you?" She says "Why?" And he says, "Well, haven't you noticed that every time the furnace goes on there are weird odours in our room?" She says, "Yeah, I did notice it, but I didn't know quite what it was."

Lonnie, he's looking at me kind of weird and I'm thinking, "What's up?" After they leave, I say, "Why were you looking at me like that?" He says, "You know why it smells in the bedroom, don't you?" I say, "No." He says, "Because there was a time that you went into the bedroom because you couldn't get in the bathroom because of all the puke, and you urinated in the reservoirs on the radiator." So I guess every time the furnace went on, there'd be this urine odour coming out of the reservoirs.

I never drank alcohol again until I was in my late thirties, and although I do enjoy an occasional cocktail and maybe have two or three beers a year, I never drink whisky. I'm a very light social drinker—most of the time it's mocktails rather than cocktails.

The thing is, my dad was a drinker. Truthfully? He wasn't just a drinker, he was an alcoholic. But he wasn't a bad alcoholic and he was never abusive, ever.

I mean, because he was playing piano in the nightclubs, he was in a world where there was a lot of smoking and drinking, so he smoked and he drank. People would come up and put a glass of beer on the table and say, "Play such and such song, Tony." He'd have his bar lined up with drinks. It was just his way of life. He drank every night, every single night. Even when he was retired from playing the nightclubs, he'd drink every night. He'd start drinking wine after dinner, watching TV, and he would drink and fall asleep. He was a lovable guy, everybody loved him, but he had no passion for life at the end.

I tried to be in a band for a while too. I actually played bass guitar in a band in my teens, but I didn't keep it up. I kept seeing my dad, thinking, "I don't want to be like this."

Plus, I actually wasn't very good.

Not like my dad. He could play everything from classical to honky-tonk. I could play a record for him, even some of my teen-age records, and I'd say, "Dad, listen to this," and he'd listen to it and he'd say, "Play it again." I'd play it again and then he'd play it on the piano as if he was reading the music. It just blew me away to see a talent like that. I really had to work at playing bass guitar. It was hard. I could do it but I didn't enjoy it, because it seemed like too much work. But Dad, he could play it just by listening to it.

And there was this song he always played for me, "Alley Cat." Whenever I'd come into the club where he was playing, it would be the very next song he'd play and he'd dedicate it to me. It always made me smile as soon as he played it. And it didn't matter where he was playing—no matter the venue—he'd play that song for me and it always made me smile.

But when it came to drinking, I went the other way. The other thing about me, too, was that when it came to smoking and drinking, I didn't really want to spend a lot of money on those kinds of things because there was so much stuff I wanted in the science shop. I couldn't understand how people could afford to spend three or four good dollars on a glass of liquid. It just didn't make sense to me. I developed this philosophy early in life that I'd rather spend my money on something tangible that's going to give me years of pleasure than watch it go down the drain or up in smoke. I did start smoking, mind you. I smoked for several years but managed to quit 25 years ago.

And, of course, I'd come from a family that didn't have a lot of money; we always had to be careful. So when I did get money, I certainly didn't want to spend it on something that was gone within minutes, especially when I could get something from the science shop like a special mounted butterfly and feel real good about looking at it over and over again. I saw more value in life than smoking and drinking and hanging around pool halls. My buddies liked doing that. They went to pool halls and they played poker a lot but they accepted that I had this other big interest in my life. The only time they got annoyed with me about it was when we went golfing, because I always hit my ball into the woods so I could lift up logs looking for animals. I'd come back with my golf bag full of creatures. They always had to wait for me to come out of the woods.

Actually, I did play poker for a little while when I was a kid. My buddies and I would play poker and we'd bet money. My sister and I got really minimal allowances from our parents, but I'd always talk her out of her allowance saying that if she gave it to me, I'd win back more money and be able to give it to her. I always lost, though. I never won at poker and she never had her allowance.

When I look back at the things I did to that poor girl . . . However, she got even later in life, one day when I wasn't expecting it. I hadn't seen her for about six years and she invited me over for dinner. I was excited to go to her place, a new apartment condo she had. I knocked at the door and I heard her yell for me to come in. I walked in and noticed there was no furniture and I didn't see her. All of a sudden the door closed. She was standing behind the door and she had a black-belt judo outfit on and she just flipped me from one end of that apartment to the other. She said, "Remember the time you threw the snake at me?" Bam! "And remember you made me stick my finger in the light socket to get the penny?" Flip! Bam! I was black and blue when I came home that day. Anyway, I guess it made her feel better. She still lives in Toronto and I'm here on the west coast, so we don't see each other often, but we talk on the phone and exchange e-mails once in a while. We laugh now about what we did in the past and she has a lot of fun talking to her friends about the tortures I used to put her through.

But as for musical talent, what talent I had went into my feet. Like my dad could hear and then play the music, I could see somebody do a dance step and get up and do it without even having to practice it. I was always the one getting girls at the dances, and I believe that was because I could dance. My buddies got me to show them how to dance too so that they wouldn't look like geeks on the dance floor. If you knew how to dance and you were cool and you had some really cool moves, then it would be easier for you to meet girls. And of course as we got older, meeting girls became more and more important, even for Lonnie.

Meeting one special girl kind of ended the crazy years, but I've always been thankful that Lonnie opened up that door for me because it might not have happened without him. I'm not saying they were all good experiences, but it was a door that I needed to go through, to experience things in life with a bit of craziness, a bit of adventure, and a bit of being the bad boy. Fact is, I love experiencing everything in life. I really do, from every emotion to every type of adventure I can get into.

I always go back to my animals—they're my security and stability in life—but I needed to do those other things and I don't regret any of it.

8 The Irenes

There was this one place we used to go to for dances, and, naturally, to meet girls. The hottest girls there were these two girls that dressed and looked identical. On top of that, both of them were named Irene. Everybody thought they were twins but they weren't even sisters. They were both Ukrainian—one was actually born in the Ukraine, but the other was Polish-Ukrainian from Germany.

That one night, one of my buddies came up to me and said, "Let's go and ask the Irenes if they want to dance." I said, "What, are you crazy? First of all they won't dance with us, second of all the guys they hang out with will probably kill us." Because they hung out with a tough group of guys and nobody messed with their girls, right? I said, "No, there's no way." He said, "Come on. You know you can dance and anyway, all they can do is say no." He bugged me and bugged me, and bugged me, you know? Halfway through the night, I finally said, "Okay, okay. Let's go. We'll ask them and then you'll be satisfied. You won't bug me anymore, right?" He goes, "Right."

So I walked up to one of them and I said, "Hi, would you like to dance?" She said "Sure," at which point I turned around and said, "Okay, thank you," and started to walk away. She said, "I said 'yes'"! I stopped and turned around and said, "Did you say yes?" And she goes, "Yeah. I'd love to dance with you." So I said, "Oh. Okay." We danced a few numbers and then a slow song came up.

I was dancing with her on the slow song and she said, "You're a really good dancer. I noticed when you were dancing with the other girls." I said, "Yeah, well, I like dancing," and she said, "Well, anytime you want to dance, you just come and ask me. I'll never turn you down." I thought, "Cool!"

I went back to my seat and I thought, "Oh my God, those guys are going to be waiting for me after the dance and they're going to beat the heck out of me." I thought, "Oh, I've really messed myself up." But you know what? I guess she said something to them. They didn't bother me.

So each week I would go to the dance and I would dance with her. We got quite close, and she eventually invited me over to her house, so I went over and we hit it off pretty good. The following week she asked me if I had any other guy friends. I said, "Yeah, why?" She said, "Because my friend Irene doesn't like your friend John." John was my buddy who had asked the other Irene to dance that time. The only guy I could think of was Lonnie so the next time I saw the two Irenes together I said, "Well, I've got this buddy, Lonnie. He's never really been with a girl, if you know what I mean. I don't think he's even kissed a girl. He's really awkward around girls and shy." My Irene said, "Well, bring him anyway. She can make her own mind up from there."

So the next week I brought Lonnie over to Irene's house. I told Lonnie, "You're going to meet this beautiful girl. This is the most beautiful girl I've ever found for you, and so blah blah blah blah, and man, you gotta really be cool on this one, you know?" And he was like, "Okay." He was starting to get a bit of an interest in girls by then.

He walks into the house and I introduce him to the girls: "Hi, this is Irene, and this is Irene." He went and sat down beside my Irene. Put his arm on the back of the couch around *my* Irene. I said, "Uh, Lonnie, come here." Lonnie said, "What?" I said, "Come here." So he came into the hallway and I said, "The other one's for you." "Oh," he said. "Oh, okay."

Anyway, she—the other Irene—she liked him! He was so different from all the guys that she'd met before—all these tough macho guys. Lonnie was so awkward, and she found a real sincere innocence about him. She liked the idea that she might be his first. For the next three years Lonnie and I dated the Irenes. We did everything together as couples.

Then, when I was nineteen, I decided I wanted to marry my Irene.

9 Married with Children

Deciding I wanted to marry Irene also meant taking on her family, and that wasn't easy. They had a traditional Ukrainian home and her father ran it with an iron fist. One time I brought Irene home about ten or fifteen minutes late and he actually took his belt off and hit me a few good whacks with it.

The first time I met Irene's parents was when she invited me for Easter dinner a few months after we started going out. I'd never met her parents, because they worked nights, so they were never there when I was over. But after we'd been going out for about five months, Irene said, "My parents want to meet you. They've heard so much about you already and they know that you're my boyfriend now and they want to meet you, so how about coming for Easter dinner?"

Now Polish and Ukrainian people have huge Easter feasts with amazing amounts of food and I knew her mother was a phenomenal cook, so I said, "Sure." Irene said, "You know what? Speak what little Polish I've taught you because they'll think it's cute." I was learning Polish from her because some of her friends were Polish and couldn't speak English too well. But I'd only learned how to say a few words—the usual greetings, you know?

So there I am at the dinner table and there's a long hallway that I can see down into the end of the kitchen. I'm sitting there and Irene's mom keeps bringing food and putting it on the table and I'm thinking, "Holy cow. When's this going to stop?" And then she finally walks toward us with this incredible-looking roasted turkey on a platter. And I think, maybe I'll be very cute and try to put a whole sentence together in Polish.

So, as she comes into the room, I say what I think is, "This is a beautiful big turkey." Well, she slams the turkey down on the table, looks hard at me and walks out. Next thing, Irene comes walking in and she says, "What did you say to my mother?" I say, "I just told her it's a beautiful big turkey."

"That's all you said?"

"Yes, but I said it in Polish."

"What did you say?"

I repeated to her what I said. Irene said, "That's not the word for turkey," and then she said the correct word in Polish. I said, "So what did I say?" She said, "You just called my mother a beautiful big whore." Oops! I guess I picked up the word from one of her friends, just got it confused. It was an honest mistake.

Anyway as time went on, I could see that despite that bad start, her mother liked me, and her sister liked me too. But her father was always cold to me, very cold. I learned that one of the reasons he didn't like me from the start was because I was Canadian.

He and his wife had met in a German concentration camp. They had the numbers on their arm signalling they were in line to go into the gas chambers. They weren't Jewish, but he had been an officer in the Polish army. I'm not sure why she had been there but they met, fell in love, and secretly got married. They made it through the war and my wife Irene was born in the POW camp after the war. While they were living in the camp, a Canadian farmer from Georgetown, Ontario came and picked out healthy men in the camp, who were then brought to Canada to become indentured labourers. In return for their passage and room and board, they were expected to work for the farmer for an entire year.

Her father came and worked to pay his own passage. and then to get enough money to bring over his wife and child. Once there, they all worked on the farm. Her mother told me working on that farm was worse than being in the concentration camp in Germany.

She said, "We were treated so poorly. There were nights that I would sneak into the barn, crawling on my belly, to steal milk

from the cows to feed Irene. So," she said, "He hates Canadians."
I was pure Canadian.

I tried real hard, though, to become the son-in-law he would
want. I even converted to Catholicism because he was very
religious, and because I knew I had to clean up for the wedding,
I went from looking like the Fonz to looking like Richie Cunning-
ham. But none of it did any good.

* * *

For a man who didn't like me, my father-in-law put on one
of the most extravagant weddings I've ever been involved in,
and I've been involved in a few now. It was huge. There were
hundreds of people there, most of whom I didn't even know.
I think he invited his whole church. I had my immediate family
and some of my other relatives there. There were six ushers and
six bridesmaids. Of course Lonnie was my best man, which was
an advantage because with his dad owning the bakery, we had a
five-tier wedding cake. That was pretty cool. But you know,
Irene's dad paid for everything, including all the booze and a huge
Ukrainian meal of perogies, cabbage rolls and kapusta (to name
a few).

The first couple of years were pretty good. We had our ups
and downs but we were doing okay. I had a pretty good job
working as a graphic artist for a company called National Cash
Register, designing business forms and logos and things like that.
It was good work and the pay was decent. Then my daughter
Shirene was born, and that was a really happy thing for all of us.
We bought a house a block away from where my in-laws lived,
and they helped us with the cost and with a lot of the renova-
tions. We built a finished basement in it and everything. And then
Tammy was born, two years later.

Tammy was a year old by the time that marriage ended.

Maybe if Irene and I hadn't lived so close to her parents it
might have been better, but they were always over. They were
really involved in our marriage. It was like being married to
everybody in the family. We had no privacy.

One thing her parents couldn't stand about me was my animals. In all fairness, I think it was her father, not her mom. She
never stood up for me, but I always felt that Irene's mom liked
me and I really liked her. But she was always silent when he was

around. He controlled everybody. And he hated me for several reasons. First, I was Canadian. Also, as it turned out, converting to Catholicism meant nothing to him. I wasn't a "real" Catholic. Finally, he hated the idea that I spent my money on animals, buying aquariums and things like that. I was still collecting insects and I had a huge collection. He must have said something to Irene, because she ended up giving me an ultimatum: either I got rid of the insects or the marriage was over. That's when I gave the collection away. I had 10,000 species in my collection. I donated some to the Royal Ontario Museum and some to friends. Many of my friends still have them to this day.

One of the things that really irked me was a time when I had caught these two little redbelly snakes. They're really small, inconspicuous snakes that are totally harmless. I had them in a terrarium, and one day I lifted up the moss to see where they were and there were babies. I was so excited. I couldn't believe I had actually reared snakes in captivity. I'd never done it before and I didn't know anybody else who had. They were really cute, too—the mothers were sort of a brown leafy colour, but the babies were born really dark with little white rings around their necks. I was thrilled.

One day soon after, I came home from work and looked at the tank and all I could see and smell was Raid. We had an argument that morning and Irene had taken a can of Raid and emptied it in the cage and killed every one of the snakes, both the mothers and all the babies.

I was very upset at this loss but also that my in-laws (read father-in-law) were, through Irene, forcing me to get rid of my animals. I finally gave the rest away, including a beautiful Peruvian guinea pig and a little baby squirrel. They were causing chaos and it was just easier to let them go.

Ever seen a baby rattlesnake?
Ever seen a whole bunch of them?

http://www.savingcinemazoo.com/episode5.html

10 Hawks and Shocks

So there we were. I wasn't happy. Irene wasn't happy. Her parents were definitely not happy. The only good things in my life at that time were my little girls and my work.

I was still working as a graphic artist and I liked the work, but mostly I liked being able to spend my lunch hours sitting in this massive field located behind the plant. Sitting out in that field, where I'd occasionally see animals and insects, was a way of keeping some connection to that part of me. It didn't take long until I discovered two red-tailed hawks nesting in a dead tree in the field.

Now red-tailed hawks are pretty unusual. They're the largest of the hawks and weigh anywhere between two and four pounds; the female is the larger of the two. Their wingspan can be as broad as 56 inches (or over one and a half yards)! Adult hawks are dark brown on their backs and tops of their wings; their undersides are usually light with a dark band across their belly and a cinnamon wash on the neck and chest. Their main feature of course are their rich russet tails that are best seen when they leave their perches and soar overhead. Let me tell you, I spent many happy lunch hours watching those hawks.

One day, though, I came back to work after a week's holiday and noticed there were two surveyors out in the field and wooden stakes in the ground all over the place. I walked out to the surveyors and said, "What's going on?" This one guy told me the field was slated to become an industrial park. It was February at the time, but he said they were about to start bulldozing and expected to have the park up and running by maybe April.

I said, "Well, what about that tree over there? Where's it going to be?" He had the blueprints right there so he looked and then he said "Well, it looks like that tree is going to be right in the middle of a factory. So it'll be coming down." I said, "Well there's a pair of Red-tailed hawks that are nesting there. That's their nest right there. You're going to take out their babies and everything?" He said "That's progress, you know. Not much we can do about it."

Well, I wasn't going to let that happen, so I started to ask around about what could be done for these hawks. I talked to some people at the Royal Ontario Museum and they said they could get somebody to help me learn a bit about falconry. I told them that I'd been reading some books on it as well, so they said, "Well, if you can get the birds and condition them and get them at least to accept being on the fist, then you could turn them over to a falconer who might want to use them for airports or whatever." I said, "Okay," and I started to get excited about it.

So I came up with a plan to capture the birds and booked some time off work to do it. I couldn't tell Irene what I was doing, so I'd get up in the morning and tell her that I was going to work. Everything looked normal—she'd take the kids to her parents on her way to her work and I'd go on my merry way to the field. I disguised myself so if anyone in the factory happened to look out the window, they wouldn't know it was me.

In February, with the help of a friend, I built a trench big enough to hold me. I had chicken wire I could put over my head. I would lay down in the trench, put the wire over my head, and put grass on it. Then I'd hold a live pigeon through the wire and grass so my hands couldn't be seen and so the pigeon couldn't get away.

My friend watched it all from his car, close enough that he could help if needed.

We wait, and wait, and then sure enough I hear *flap! flap! flap!* I'm trying to see through this mesh and hold the pigeon and all of a sudden *BAM!* This hawk hits the pigeon.

I grab the hawk's legs and hold him and he's flapping like crazy and I finally sit up and I put my arm around his wing and I'm holding him and my friend runs to join me and we get a sock over the top of the hawk's head so he can't fly or see or anything, and then we put him in the car. Then we set it all up again.

Well, the pigeon is half-dead by now, so I'm having to move it around to make it look like it's still alive. I lie there for another two hours on the frozen ground—blue and shivering so hard I'm sure I'll give myself away—but finally, down the male comes and grabs the pigeon. I'm only able to grab the hawk by one leg this time. What a battle to get him! Fortunately, I had thick gloves on.

Finally I had them both. I had nowhere else to take them, so I took them home. I knew I'd have to hide them, but my father-in-law had built a root cellar in the basement of our house under the stairs and I figured that would be the place. There were shelves on each side of the room, and so I put a board across the two shelves and put the birds up on top of that. I tied them to the board. Frankly, I really didn't know what I was doing, but I knew enough to turn the lights off because I figured making it pitch black in there would be equivalent to the hood that hawks wear to calm them down and keep them quiet when they're in captivity.

Once they were secure, I left so I could go out of the house and then come back in, pretending that I was coming home from work as usual. My plan was to have a normal quiet evening, you know, play with the kids, have dinner, go to bed. Then when I got up in the morning, I'd take another day off work and go around the neighbourhood looking for a garage for rent where I could put the hawks. Then I could start training them.

Good plan. Not what happened.

Next morning, I found the garage I needed and rented it. I returned to the house about 1:00 in the afternoon and lo and behold, the front door was unlocked. I thought "Oh geez, did I forget to lock the door this morning?" I walked in the house and it was quiet so I went to the kitchen and made myself a sandwich and then walked downstairs towards the root cellar.

When I got down there what do I see but my mother-in-law's feet sticking out of the root cellar. My heart was in my mouth. As soon as I got closer and saw her breathing, I knew she wasn't dead. But I was.

She had a key to the house and she had come in to get some preserves from the root cellar. When she flicked on the light these two birds went *squawk! squawk!* and were flying around flapping their wings. And remember, they have a huge wingspan. She fainted, right? And she fell face-first into the root cellar.

I didn't think she was hurt but the part that was the worst was that I couldn't crawl over her to get to her head. She was a big woman and she filled the doorway. And the birds had obviously defecated on her head, so she had a couple of big splotches of bird poop on the back of her head.

I thought, "Oh my God, I've got to get her out of here." So I picked her up by her ankles and I started pulling her out and as I was pulling her out, her skirt was going up over her behind. I . . . really didn't want to see that.

So I'm looking away as I'm pulling her out, and who should appear at the top of the stairs but Irene, who has for some reason come home early this day. The birds had been making so much noise I hadn't heard her.

Irene sees me holding her mother's ankles at the root cellar door and she screams the most blood-curdling scream I've ever heard. I drop my mother-in-law's feet and look up at Irene, who yells, "You killed my mother!" And then she runs off.

So I'm running after her trying to explain, saying, "No, she fainted. Come back and help me." Finally she believes me, and we come back. The birds are screeching and Irene is all in a panic.

"What are they doing here?"

"I'm taking them out right now. They were just here temporarily and they scared your mother. And you know . . . "

So we finally get her mother out and her mom's moaning and groaning. Irene is crying. Then her mother is crying. And now they're talking rapidly to each other in Polish. I don't know what they're saying, but I know they're not happy. And then, the next thing I know, her father shows up. Things are getting really bad.

I say, "Look, I've got to get these birds out of here."

So I turned the lights out and calmed the birds down. I got a towel over them and wrapped them up, put them in a sack, and took them to the garage I'd found and set them up there. Then I came back to the house.

Nobody was home. Everything was quiet. I phoned my in-laws' place and there was nobody there, no answer. So then I walked up the block to their house and knocked on the door and again, no answer. And the lights were all out. I couldn't figure out where they could all have gone, so I decided to go back home and just wait until they showed up.

I remember sitting down and watching the hockey game, and then, right near the end of the game, I heard someone at the front door. My sister-in-law came in first, then my father-in-law, who looked at me like he was going to kill me. My wife came in right behind my mother-in-law, who came in on crutches because when I'd dropped her feet I'd broken her toe.

Then they started at me. They were calling me every name in the book and it was all in Polish, of course. I knew what some of them were. One of them definitely had to do with a pig's venereal disease. In Polish, that's the worst thing that you can have. I remember that well.

After listening to as much as I could take, I just said, "You know what? You guys don't understand me at all and I'm going to bed. Good night." And I walked in the bedroom and went to sleep.

The next morning, I got up and went to work. They were all still at our house so I just ignored them, got ready, and went to work. Before coming home that day, I stopped by the garage to make sure the birds were okay because I had to leave them for a few days to settle down.

When I got back to the house, there were a few neighbours standing around the fence in front of my property. I got out of my car and walked up the sidewalk and then saw that everything I owned was on the front lawn. I knew that was it. I never said a word. I just loaded up my car, put everything in it. The only thing I said to Irene was: "I guess we'll be talking about things later." She said, "That's right." And so I left

***

For the next couple of weeks I lived in the garage with the birds, then I moved back in with my parents for a bit. Around the same time, I got laid off from the graphic design job. It was not a good period in my life.

I was only allowed to visit my daughters for one hour on Sundays. It was very difficult. It seemed like every time I came, I'd be told the girls were sick or teething or there was some other reason they couldn't come out with me. If they could come out, we were constrained by having only one hour to visit.

Eventually, I moved to a farm and then not only did it take over an hour to drive to pick them up, but the grandparents and their mother didn't want the girls around the farm animals. And, after awhile, I had no money so I got several months behind on child-support payments.

Finally my wife called and said they wanted to talk with me. I said, "Okay."

So I showed up and Irene, interpreting for her father, said, "Here's the deal." He wanted me to give up seeing the kids altogether or he was going to take me to court and sue me and garnish any job I ever got for my money. He basically laid it on the line that if I agreed not to see the girls anymore and left the raising of the kids to them and my wife, he would not do these punitive things and I would not have to pay child support. I was to walk away and never come back.

He also said, "What is going on right now is not good for the kids. You pick them up. You keep them out for an hour. You bring them back and you cry." I would cry because I didn't want to take them home. I wanted more time with them. And he said, "They see you upset and they get upset. It's not good for the kids."

In the end, he convinced me. I thought about it for a couple of days and I phoned up Irene and I said, "I agree." I knew that they would be raised well and that what was happening now was not good for them. But it was very hard.

I mean, I love my daughters like anything. In the first few years of not seeing them, I'd come and sit at the top of their street and look at them with binoculars so I could see what they looked like. I'd watch them coming in and out of the house, maybe going to school. But I stayed far enough away that no one would know I was there. I was afraid of him and what he might do.

I spent a lot of years crying about them, dreaming about them and things like that. I kept dreaming that some day it was going to change. I'd get to know them and they'd get to know me and I was sure when they did they were going to be happy they did. It took 15 years for that to happen. The day it did was one of the most memorable days in my life.

***

I saw my daughters again 15 years later. I'd gone back to Toronto to be with my dad, who was dying. I made it just in time and was able to be with him when he died. He and I were alone and I had just shown him a painting. He saw it and smiled and took a breath, and that was it.

My mother and my sister came by and I told them that he had just passed on. After comforting each other, we spent the rest of the morning going through some things he had at the hospital, and then headed home.

To my great surprise, Lonnie came over! I hadn't seen him for years. He knew I was coming and I guess he knew my dad was sick but I didn't tell him Dad had just died. It didn't seem appropriate at the time.

Lonnie said, "How about coming out for lunch with me right now?" I said, "Yeah, maybe that's a good idea," because I wanted to get away from all the sadness in the house. I hadn't cried at Dad's passing, because frankly I was glad his misery was over. He died of cancer after going from 250 pounds to 87 pounds. It was horrible to see him like that, knowing there was no chance of recovery whatsoever. At least his death was peaceful; I'd been hoping for a peaceful death.

Anyway, Lonnie—who was in great spirits—said "Come on out. I've got a special spot I want to take you for lunch," and I said, "Sure."

So we hop in the car and we drive to this little plaza and there's a Shoppers Drug Mart, I remember, and a restaurant right next to it. We go into the restaurant and I'm following Lonnie because he knows where he's going, and we get up to this booth and I look in the booth and there's these two girls sitting there. I know right away, "Oh my God. It's my daughters!" Lonnie says, "I thought I'd give you a bit of a surprise."

What a surprise! I mean, like, my emotions were going nuts that day, you know? I didn't have the heart to tell them that Dad had just died earlier that day and that I was going through all these emotions.

It was a really a strange encounter. The girls, who would have been in their late teens at that time, were very curious to know more about me. They'd wanted to meet me but didn't tell their mom and their grandparents that they were coming out to meet me. Their mom wouldn't have said anything, but their grandfather was still totally against it, He cut all my pictures out of all the wedding shots and everything as if I was some kind of a criminal or something. The irony is that the worst thing I ever did in those days was smoke. Oh, and have animals and be a Canadian and not a natural-born Catholic . . . come to think of it, I guess I had a lot of strikes against me.

But it was a good meeting. It was so good to see them. They said, "You know, I hope you don't mind that we call you Gary because we just . . . we've never known you as anything else, you know?"

We went to the zoo and had a fun day there and then we went riding out at the farm I'd shared with my second wife, Sylvia, who was—and is still—a friend. It was a good day.

We've kept in touch over the years, and now Tammy, the youngest, wants to come out here and be a part of my life. And guess what? She's a total animal nut. Sherry, a beautiful woman with two beautiful kids, has a good job in Toronto, so she'll probably stay there, but she wants to come out and visit.

When they were young, nobody was allowed to talk about me in the family. Their grandfather died some time ago and after he was no longer around to control things, they told me that their Grandma said, "Gary wasn't a bad man. He was a really interesting person and people liked him."

I never gave up believing that I would get to know my daughters someday—I just knew it would happen. It's exciting. Now they're starting to learn more and more. They're not resentful toward their grandparents or their mom, they're just really curious to know more about me and so far they say they like what they see.

One thing is for sure: the end of that marriage marked a major turning point in my life.

11 Sylvia
and the Ranch Years

I couldn't survive forever on unemployment insurance, nor did I want to. Eventually I got hired on as a bingo caller at the CNE (the Canadian National Exhibition) in Toronto. That was how I met Sylvia.

Sylvia was my supervisor. She was a few years older than me and was married with seven kids, but we soon became good friends. We shared an interest in animals, especially the horses at the Horse Palace right across from the bingo hall. Sylvia and I would go there on our coffee breaks and during the lunch hour, and we'd watch the horses and talk about horses the whole time.

I wasn't real knowledgeable, but I loved them and had volunteered at a stable when I was a kid. When I got older I used to rent horses to ride. I always felt comfortable on them and maybe that's because I could dance. I think having a good sense of rhythm, being able to pick up a beat in dancing or whatever, makes for a better rider. And, of course, riding the steers at the slaughterhouse undoubtedly helped.

Anyway, because she knew how much I loved them, Sylvia encouraged me to get a horse. She had a farm and she said I could keep it at her stable and she wouldn't charge me for it. She just wanted to see me have a horse.

I went up to a place called the Hockey Ranch in Pickering, Ontario, just up the road from Sylvia's farm. You could pick out any horse you wanted there and lease it for a season.

I picked out this beautiful black horse and rode it back to Sylvia's stable about a kilometre and a half away. Thing was, it had the weirdest gait and I couldn't figure out why. I'd never felt a gait like it before. I thought maybe it was me, that I just wasn't able to pick up the horse's beat. It felt kind of silly riding that horse, the way it was moving.

Anyway, I reached the farm and Sylvia and I went out for a ride. As soon as she saw the horse move, she started laughing. "You idiot," she said. "You picked out a pacer!" I think I said, "Oh." She said, "Yeah, they move the same legs on the same side—a kind of back-and-forth motion. You're not going to be able to learn really good horsemanship on that."

So, back to the Hockey Ranch we went and this time I picked out a little horse named Lone Star. This horse could do everything. When I became more used to riding her, and became a better rider, I used to do trick riding on Lone Star. I'd gallop down the lawn in front of Sylvia's house and the kids would pretend to shoot me and I'd fall off and do these stunt falls. Lone Star would come back and roll me over. God, I loved that horse.

I had all kinds of fun with Lone Star. I did jumping and even entered into shows, riding both English and Western. When the lease ended and I had to bring her back to the Hockey Ranch, I asked them if I could buy her, but they wouldn't sell her to me.

The sad story is two months later I went up to the Hockey Ranch again to see if maybe I could convince them to sell Lone Star. My parents came with me because they were going to help me buy the horse. But the people at the Ranch said they didn't have her. I said, "Where is she?" And they said Lone Star had gone to Picot Downs—a big quarter horse racetrack and meat dealer. They said Lone Star was down in the meat farm. So my parents and I went down there.

We found Lone Star standing in a stall, totally foundered. Foundering is what happens when horses are left standing in poor conditions, like wet soggy ground. The feet rot. The hoof bones actually begin to work their way through the skin on the hoof.

Lone Star couldn't walk and it was obvious she was in agony. I felt so sorry for her, I cried. She was so far gone there was nothing that could be done for her. All I could hope was that they would put her down quickly so she wouldn't suffer much longer.

***

Sylvia and I kept riding and I was spending more and more time at the farm. This meant a commute for me of about 160 kilometres a day so I could ride my horse, and in the winter, this meant a long drive for a short ride because there was so little daylight left by the time I got out there.

Sylvia thought it was crazy that I was doing all this driving and decided to talk to her husband about having me board with them. They and their seven kids lived in this amazing big old heritage home that was at least a century old. Originally it had been one of several buildings that were part of a Quaker community.

Their house was known as the East Heritage but there were also the West, the South, North and the Central Heritage houses. The Central house used to be a Quaker college and it had a big hall with wooden floors and large fireplaces located at each end. The fireplaces were roughly seven feet high, topped by huge mantels, and above each mantel was a relief. One of the reliefs was of the ship the *Mayflower*, and the other was of an Indian brave teaching his son how to draw an arrow through a bow. It was fantastic.

Every spring, the fellow who managed the Heritages would stoke up the fires and keep them burning for three days to get heat into the building, and then he'd invite everyone in the neighbourhood to celebrate Robbie Burns Day. They'd pipe in the haggis and have a huge party. It was the first time I'd ever tasted haggis and probably the first time I'd ever heard of Robbie Burns. It was sure a lot of fun.

Anyway, there was a lot of room in their house and even though they had seven kids, Sylvia thought I could board with the family or at least stay over on the weekends. Her husband agreed, and I moved in. I shared a room with her youngest and two of the older boys doubled up.

I really loved living there. We had great times. It was just like living with the Waltons. There were huge gatherings every meal—often with people I didn't even know. "Whatever your name is, pass the potatoes, please!"

In the morning, I'd get up to go to the bathroom and there'd be a line-up to get into the one bathroom in the house because the kids were getting ready for school. Sylvia would have been up long before. She didn't work, but she'd be out seeing to the horses.

Anyway, I'd be standing in line and there would be kids standing next to me that I didn't know. They'd be friends of Sylvia's kids who'd come over and ended up staying the night. Frankly, I always thought it was a rip-off that I didn't have seniority when it came to the bathroom! And it would be cold standing in that hallway in the winter because of course there was no central heating. There were two space heaters in the house: one in the kitchen and one in the dining room. Everyone congregated in the kitchen and we spent as much time there as possible. I saw many snowsuits get burned on that stove. People would put the snowsuit on the stove to warm it up and then forget about it. Next thing you know, there'd be a big burn patch on it.

It could get so cold in that house that you'd have to break the ice in the toilet to use it. And then the kids would wash the dishes and leave the water in the sink and it would freeze, or the water would freeze in the pipes. I can remember many times standing outside the house with a propane torch, heating the water pipes so we could get the water running in the kitchen and get the sink to drain. But you know, we had a lot of fun in that house; no doubt about it.

Gord—Sylvia's husband—was a great guy, but he was never around. He'd ask me to fill in for him on many occasions like taking Sylvia to horse shows (or banquets having to do with horse shows). If he didn't want to see a movie and she did, he'd ask me to take her. Several times I took the family out for dinner, and with seven kids ranging in age from one to fifteen, that could be expensive. I always paid. I wasn't expected to, but to this day, if I take someone out for dinner, I pay.

Well—perhaps not surprisingly given the amount of time we were spending together—Sylvia and I became very fond of each other. She was, and is, a great woman and although she's maybe ten years older than me, she looked like one of the kids back then. She certainly looked as young as I did. People would meet us as a group and wonder who these two older kids were with all the younger kids. They couldn't believe that these seven kids belonged to us, and I would have to point out that they did not actually belong to me.

One day in the spring—I'd been living there for several months—Gord came up to me and said, "Can we go for a walk?" I was sort of concerned because I figured he was going to confront me about my relationship with Sylvia. You can imagine my surprise when instead of confronting me, he told me he was going to leave the marriage. He could see how close Sylvia and I had become and he just thought it was better for him to move on.

I said, "If you're leaving because of me, I should be the one to move on because I don't want to be responsible for your family breaking up." He said, "Gary, you're the best thing that ever happened to this family. I don't share Sylvia's love for horses and animals like you do, and you relate well to the kids and the kids really love you because you take time with them. You do things with them." I felt like saying "Yeah, but that's because I'm still a kid myself." "Also," he said, "my wife loves you and I know you're fond of her. This is something that's been going through my mind for quite a while. It's a tough decision, but I really feel you're the best person for this family. Just promise me that you'll take good care of them, that's all I ask." He told me he'd discussed it with Sylvia and they'd agreed it was best he leave.

What he didn't tell me was that he was leaving a whole bunch of debts. Gord had a good job and made decent money, but he did have a drinking problem. In fact, the only time I had a problem with him was one time when he got a bit drunk and threatened me with a gun. I finally calmed him down and then locked him up in the tack room. He was pretty upset the next morning that he'd done that. Anyway, he hadn't paid the rent on the house for several months and there were other bills that hadn't been paid. Fortunately, I inherited a bit of money at that time and I was able to clear up the debts. I also got my first credit card and started building my own debts because the family needed things like a new fridge and stove.

So there I was, not yet 25, and I had a family with seven children. I was a bit in shock when Gord made his announcement, but I found that I did love Sylvia and I loved the kids. Like I said, they were a great family.

▲ My great-grandfather and me in Longbranch, Ontario, just a short time before all the homes on that street were swept away into Lake Ontario by a massive flood

►My first stint in the militia!
A true cub, Toronto, Ontario

▲ My Uncle Ted and Aunt Marie's cottage in Keswick, Ontario, on Lake Simcoe, where I brushed shoulders with my first celebrities. I actually rode on John Wayne's shoulders and I met Peter Graves, Johnny Weismüller, Rocky Marciano and Whipper Billy Watson. But, to me as a kid, they were just my uncles.

◄ At 16, my second stint in the forces. Got my first glimpse of Queen Elizabeth II in 1963

▲ In my bedroom on Bloor Street, Toronto, Ontario 1966

▲ Lonnie, Irene, Irene and me at the Hawk's Nest
on Younge Street, Toronto, Ontario 1966

▲ June 29th, 1973. That's me as a Governor General's Horse Guard, escorting Queen Elizabeth II and Prince Phillip at the Queen's Plate Race, Woodbine, Ontario

► I'm 3rd from the left at the opening of the Provincial Legislature in Toronto, 1972.

▼ One of our Arabians and me at Hy-Az-A-Kyte Farm, Aldergrove, BC. 1976

▲ Mural of the Workers' Waterfront in Vancouver, by Fraser Wilson in 1947. When it was moved to the Maritime Labour Auditorium in 1988, it was shortened from 98 to 82 feet

▼ Gary and his dog Jason in front of the mural he helped to save

▲ Open house at the Pacific Artists Studio, 337 West Pender

▼ The Pacific Artists Studio, 1979–1990.
My Mom's art supply store, McEwen's Arts, is on the right.

▲ Another of my favourite felines—notice the ressemblance

12 Bringing Home the Bacon

Considering how Gord hadn't been around much anyway, life at the farm continued pretty much as it had before, except that Sylvia and I were now sharing a bed.

I got my job as a graphic artist with the National Cash Register Company back, which helped pay the bills, and Sylvia took care of the horse-breeding business. Plus we had a few other animals, like Myrtle the pig.

Myrtle is worth a story or two.

She was just a regular pig that we bought to raise for the fridge, but we kind of got attached to her. She became like one of the dogs around the farm—she'd follow us around and after a while, she became a house pet. She never messed in the house, but she did get pretty big, pretty fast because she not only got her regular food, but also a lot of our leftovers from the table. Came a point we had to move her out to the barn. There were actually several barns on this property, arranged in a horseshoe pattern around a central paddock. Myrtle's favourite spot was the stud barn with the horses. She used to wander around that barn, and the horses liked her. She'd go out to the pasture with them and everything. I'm not sure why, but she kept them calm.

One of my favourite Myrtle stories is from the time Sylvia had some people coming up to look at one of the stallions we had for sale. Sylvia suggested it might be a good idea to move Myrtle out of the stud barn and into one of the other barns that these people would not be going into. I said, "Sure, yeah, okay."

Now I mentioned that the barns were arranged around a paddock. There was a gate that went into that paddock, and the paddock itself was pretty mucky because our manure pile was in there. Trucks would come in every once in a while to clean up the manure, but they hadn't been there for a while so at that time the pile was pretty high.

So I put a rope around Myrtle's neck and start walking her out of the barn. We get half way through the mud and the manure and she decides she doesn't want to go any further. I try to get her to move and the rope slips off. I grab her around the neck and try to lead her away but she resists, and she is big—she weighs a few hundred pounds by now. Finally, we fall, and we're rolling around in the mud. I have to confess, it's fun. Myrtle's tossing me all over the place and I'm killing myself laughing.

The next thing I know, I'm lying on my side with my legs wrapped around Myrtle's waist. She's on her side and I have my arms around her neck and we're soaking wet. There are flies, mud and manure everywhere. We're both exhausted and we're lying there panting and sweating—having a break—and just then Sylvia comes walking by with the people who'd come to see the stallion.

Sylvia is saying, "Yes, these are our three barns. We keep our fillies over here, we keep some of our stock over here, and the stallion barn is over there." And then she looks over into the centre and sees Myrtle and me lying in the mud and the manure, and she says, "And this is my husband and our pet, Myrtle," without breaking stride, like all's perfectly normal, and just keeps walking by us. In the meantime, the people with her are looking at me like "What have we gotten ourselves into?"

Like I said, Sylvia was pretty cool. (We were in fact married by then. We were married by the captain of the Governor General's Horse Guards—another door, another story to come).

One morning the kids went down to the barn to do their chores. They came running back into the house crying, "Myrtle's not here! She's gone! She's not in the field—we can't find her anywhere!"

We looked all over the farm. Myrtle was nowhere to be found.

A block away from the farm was a fairly new subdivision and I thought maybe she might have wandered off there, so I started driving through it, but there was no sign of her there either.

Now you have to remember this is a big pig. By then she was somewhere around seven, maybe eight hundred pounds, if not more. Not easy for her to hide. Still, I couldn't find her anywhere. I was driving around and around, going up the country road that ran beside our place, looking in the fields, looking everywhere.

I had the radio on in the car and I heard: "Will the owner of a pig please come to Pickering Village to the McKechran Funeral Home. Your pig has been found."

So I drove back to the farm and picked up Sylvia and I said, "They found her, it was on the radio and apparently she's at the funeral home." The funeral home was a little over three kilometres from the farm.

Well, we get to the funeral home, and lo and behold: she's in the garage, wedged between the hearse and the wall, and she can't turn around. The police and the funeral home guys don't want to move the hearse in case she gets a leg caught in the wheel or whatever. So I get in behind her, between the hearse and the wall, and I just keep backing her up until we get her out.

We all laugh about how this pig went to market and ended up in a funeral home. Wait, the story's not over!

At that time, I had a '61 Chevy Bel Air—a four-door. So I opened up the back door and she got in. She took up the whole back seat. I had to force the door closed because she was more than the seat could hold.

We're driving back down the highway towards our farm and I see in the rear-view mirror that she's put her head up in the back window-well and is basically filling up the whole window. Two seconds later, I swear, I see in my side mirror that there's a red flashing light and I get pulled over by the highway police. I think, "Well, I'm not speeding. I wonder what the heck he wants?"

So I pull over, and he walks up to the car, looks in the back window and says, "I just wanted to make sure I was seeing what I was seeing." And I said, "Yeah, this is the pig that was stuck in the funeral home." He goes, "Okay, now I know who it is. I just wanted to make sure you weren't trying to give me some kind of an insult, you know?" I said, "No-o-o." He laughed and said, "Okay. Take it easy, folks," and took off.

About a month later though, we had to get her slaughtered. I guess she'd had too much of a taste of being on the road and she started breaking fences. It was sad for all of us, but she was the best ham I ever had. I mean, no doubt about it, we fed her right.

13 Foreshadowing

I was still very interested in insects during these years, but living on a farm gave me a chance to learn more about larger animals, which was great. Fact is, I love animals of all kinds, and ever since this guy came to my school and talked about animals when I was eight years old, I've known I wanted to work with animals.

So you can imagine how excited I was when Joe Lucas moved in next door to our farm. Joe had just been hired to be the curator and director for the new Toronto Metropolitan Zoo (still in construction at the time).

It was going to be an innovative zoo. They had all these new concepts for moats and things like that—more of an open plan. Joe asked if we could do a couple of favours for him. First, the zoo was bringing in some animals that would need to be quarantined for a period of time and he wondered if he could use one of our barns for this. I said, "Sure, no problem." The other thing he needed was a place to keep his dog Simba while he got settled because it was going to take him a while to get everything organized. He was going to be travelling back and forth and didn't know what to do with Simba during this period. He asked if we could keep the dog for a bit. I said, "Sure."

Simba was a beautiful Rhodesian Ridgeback from Africa—one of the biggest I've ever seen in my life, a massive dog. Joe had been a game warden in Africa and he told me that Simba had been used on actual lion hunts. I remember that Simba would put his head in your lap and just leave it there. Nice . . . except let me tell you, there was no way you could get up if he'd done that. If you tried, he would growl, and with this huge head in your lap pointing toward your belly, you weren't about to take any chances. So you just sort of patted him until he got bored and he would leave.

We kept our doors open, and because the place was well fenced, Simba had freedom to roam throughout the farm. He could go in and out of the house or sleep in the barns if he wanted.

He was a wonderful dog. The kids were great with him and he was good with everyone. We were sorry to lose him when Joe came to say that he was ready to take Simba home.

Several days later, Simba showed up at our fence line bleeding like anything. Blood was everywhere. It was during the day and Joe wasn't home so I hooked up a leash to Simba and walked him back to Joe's place, where I could see that the dog had broken through Joe's front picture window. I phoned Joe and we agreed I'd take Simba to the vet. He got a few stitches and then I took him back home.

A few days later, Simba did it again—he went through the replacement picture window. Joe's said, "What's going on with him? He's never done that." This time it took a lot of stitches to sew him up—he was stitched from one end to the other. They kept him at the clinic until the stitches could be taken out and he healed.

Joe decided he'd put Simba in a back bedroom in the house. This bedroom had a window that was too high for Simba to reach. Joe came home every day at noon to walk Simba, but he figured the dog would be safe in this room until he got home.

Not long after this, I was over working with a horse that I kept in a barn at Joe's place. I heard this crash and thought, "Oh no, not again." I went around to the front of the house and was thankful to see that there was no broken window. So I'm standing there and I'm thinking, "Where's the dog? What did he smash?" I go around to the back of the house and there I see blood all down the side of the house. Following the trail of blood up, I can see that it led from the window in that back bedroom, which was broken through.

I found Simba on the ground. He had obviously managed to jump up to the window but apparently had not made it right through. Stuck on the frame, he had pulled himself through the broken glass until he fell out. In the process, he'd severed an artery and was now losing enormous amounts of blood.

I called Joe and he rushed home but by the time he arrived, Simba was almost gone. The vet came and put Simba down. He figured Simba had been suffering from claustrophobia, probably stemming from his long period in quarantine. It was sad for all of us, but Joe had raised Simba from a puppy and losing him hurt Joe a lot.

Over time, I got to know Joe quite well. In fact, I ended up doing my first bit of actual zoo work for him.

At that point, the new Metropolitan zoo still hadn't opened for business and they were running into a problem with some of the animals—like the monkeys and baboons—escaping from their compounds. The zoo management was designing more secure compounds, but in the meantime they needed to round up the loose animals, most of whom were making their new homes in a valley at the edge of the zoo property. Zoo security figured the best way to round up the animals was to have someone on horseback go into the valley and chase them out. Joe asked me if I'd be interested in taking on the job. Not surprisingly, I said, "Sure, no problem!"

So I did that. I worked at the zoo for a couple of months.

The first time my horse saw a monkey, he just turned around immediately and began to hightail it home. I finally got him going back in the right direction, but his reaction made me realize that I needed to do some prep work. Monkeys were the most common animal we chased. So from that point on, any horse I was riding I would first ride around the monkey compounds to get it used to the monkeys. It wasn't long before the monkeys didn't bother the horse anymore. They'd scream at it but the noise wouldn't faze the horse. So then the horse and I would just herd them back.

Then Joe said, "Well, do you want to come and be part of the zoo? You can sort of assist me." I never went on the payroll, but Joe would give me money and I would come and help him out.

I got to do so many cool things; things I had never dreamed of doing with animals, like bottle-feeding gorillas and handling the big snakes, herding animals from place to place, and helping the zookeepers. I learned a lot and I enjoyed it immensely. Little did I realize at the time that I'd be doing this kind of stuff on my own later in my life. At that time, Cinemazoo wasn't even a concept in my mind. Looking back on it now, it was such good preparation for what I do today. I really appreciate that opportunity.

Overall, that was a good time in my life. People had warned me I was nuts to take on a family that size, but I was happy. I was back in the world of animals and I was spending my time with good people doing healthy things. It got even better when I got into the Governor General's Horse Guards.

14 The Governor General's Horse Guards

If you think about how much I love horses and remember that being a Mounted Policeman was one of my main ambitions as a child, you'll understand why I considered it such an honour to be part of the Governor General's Horse Guards. That is if you know anything about the Horse Guards.

The Guards date back to 1810, when they were first formed in Upper Canada as a volunteer cavalry militia known as the Markham Troop—part of a larger infantry battalion. By 1839, the Troop became independent of the battalion and formed itself as the Governor General's Body Guards, gaining regimental status in 1889. Then, in 1936, the Body Guards amalgamated with another horse unit to become the Governor General's Horse Guards, or GGHG.

The regiment has seen active duty throughout its history. They fought in the War of 1812; they chased back the American Irish Republican Army (or "Fenians") when they tried to invade Canada in 1886. They fought in the Riel Rebellion, in the second Boer War, and in both World Wars, as well as taking part in various UN peacekeeping duties.

In 1941 the regiment became mechanized, losing its horses, but when the war ended and thoughts could once again turn to matters of culture and tradition, moves were made to keep the cavalry tradition alive. Several members of the regiment formed the GGHG Riding Club, later formalized as the Governor General's Horse Guards Cavalry Squadron. The Squadron, made up of both civilian and military members, is still seen at regimental, state and civic parades; they provide mounted guards and participate in musical rides. When you see a full-dress horse escort for members of the royalty, or the Governors General and Lieutenant Governors, you are looking at members of the GGHG Cavalry Squadron.

You bet I was proud to be asked to be part of this tradition. I'd wanted to be part of it since I was 16 and belonged to the 48th Highlanders, a well-known regimental reserve unit in Toronto. I thought that was pretty good, too. The Highlanders also formed honour guards but we were on foot, more like the Black Watch. I was proud of being in the Highlanders. Once, I remember, we did an escort for the Queen; it was the first time I'd ever seen her. We wore kilts, which made us different from other reserve units, and we wore those big ostrich feather hats. It was kind of cool. And I always felt good marching behind the bagpipes.

My first glimpse of the Horse Guards was when I was at a Highlanders training camp up in Georgetown, near Niagara Falls. One of the events during the two weeks I was there required all the different divisions to march to this big church square where we would break off into our own denominations. I remember it well.

We marched to the square, led by our pipe band like all the divisions, but then we were told to wait.

We're waiting and waiting and it's a beautiful hot summer day and finally I ask, "What are we waiting for?" I'm told that the Governors General haven't shown up, and I go, "Oh, okay." I don't know who the Governors General are.

All of a sudden we hear this horrible noise down the road, and there they are. Nobody in their pipe band is playing the same tune and they're still getting dressed while they march.

We learned later that they had been out the night before and had tied one on and were having a hard time getting up and getting organized. But what impressed me more than anything was the fellow who was leading the group. He was in full regimental uniform on a horse, practically the same uniform as the Queen's Guards had in England. I thought to myself, "Oh man, I'd rather be in that regiment than the 48th Highlanders. That guy gets to ride a horse." It was so cool.

So, when I got the chance to be a Guard, I jumped at it. Another day I remember well. I had been show jumping in an equestrian show, riding a horse named Tagday. We'd had a great day. Tagday was really on his mark that day and was taking the jumps with ease. He was a terrific horse. The only problem with Tagday was that every time I went over a jump, he would fart. I had a lot of people tell me I was cheating because I was getting jet propulsion over the jumps. We cleaned up that day but to be honest with you, he was an embarrassing horse to ride.

Anyway, this guy Collin came up to me and said, "Gary, I didn't know you were such a good rider." I thanked him and then he said, "Would you like to join the Governor General's Horse Guards?"

I went, "Would I! I'm there. Let's go!"

***

I rode with the Horse Guards for many years and absolutely loved it. There was such camaraderie, but it wasn't only the friendship: the training we got in the Horse Guards was the best equine riding training I've ever had.

I can remember . . . we would have to ride at a canter and go over a series of small jumps with no saddle. In the beginning we were allowed to ride using reins, but later on we had to make the jumps with our arms out to the side: no reins, no saddle, and with two five-dollar bills between our knees. If you dropped the bills—and they were your bills—the drill sergeant kept them. And it wasn't only riding; we also had to learn things like how to take a double bridle apart, clean it, and put it back together. And to make sure that you really understood the procedure, you had to do it blindfolded. Let me tell you, that was difficult, especially trying to figure out things like how to identify the chinstraps.

It was great training and it was great fun. Being in the Guards opened up opportunities and experiences I still treasure today.

I remember this one time we did an escort for the Queen Mother. We had to take her from the Fairmont Royal York hotel in Toronto and up University Avenue to the Legislative Building for some kind of event. On the way up University Avenue there was some construction, and they had put this great big metal plate across the road—I guess to cover a hole that they had dug. My horse was a big horse—about 15 hands high—and when he got to it, his shoes hit that metal and the clanking must have spooked him a bit. His feet went out from underneath him and down we went.

He landed on his side—on my left leg—and then scrambled up to his feet with me still in the saddle, holding onto it and the four reins with my left hand and holding the sword we carried in my right. We just trotted on ahead and got back into the line.

When we were back in line, I glanced down and could see that the sheath (or "scabbard") for my sword had been bent in the fall so I couldn't put my sword back in it when it was time to do so. I could also feel my leg throbbing and throbbing. I thought to myself, "Oh my God, I've done some damage. I know I have." But I stayed on the horse in formation until the event came to a close and we escorted her back to the Royal York. Fortunately, there was no grate on our side of the road on the return journey.

At the hotel, the procedure was that the Queen Mother would be helped from her Landau—the type of horse-drawn carriage used for these occasions—and then she would walk along a red carpet up to the hotel. A few of us stood alongside the red carpet, and I happened to be closest to the Landau at that time. One of the officers in the Landau tried to open the door, but he was having problems with it, so an RCMP officer standing outside the carriage—wearing the full-dress scarlet serge tunic—tried wiggling it and pulling it, but it still stuck. All the time, everyone was trying to be graceful about it because we were on camera.

Suddenly the Queen Mother, who was sitting close to the door, said "Let me have a go at it," and I think she put the boot to it. The door flung wide open and hit the other side of the carriage, which spooked my horse. He reared straight up in the air and scrambled around. Finally, he came down, and I managed to stay on him again. I was thinking to myself, "I'm not having a good ride today," when just then the Queen Mother got out of the Landau and walked up to me. She said, "I am so sorry, young man." I said, "It's okay, your Majesty." And then she said, "Good piece of riding." I loved her. She was great.

My leg was still throbbing. When we got back to our stables and they pulled the boot off me, it turned out that it was scraped all along the side—there was a good layer of skin gone and my boot was full of blood.

All in all, it was an experience I won't forget.

But one of the funniest things that happened . . . okay.

We used to do the Queen's Plate race every year, because

there always needed to be dignitaries present for official duties like handing the wreath to the winning horse. It would be our job to act as escorts in these kinds of situations, and so for four days we'd be at the track. It was a pretty good deal. We had a mess tent where we would eat, with all the food supplied by the jockey club. The food was phenomenal. You could have steak every meal if you wanted. Another tent was set up as a canteen for those who wanted to drink. I was always with the horses, but every now and then I would go to the canteen just to socialize with everybody.

Well, I remember this one guy, Gary, had spent too much time in the canteen and had too much to drink. About two o'clock in the morning, he passed out in the canteen tent. So, for a joke, a bunch of the guys got a stretcher, put him on it and hauled him out to the warm-up track. They propped him up butt-naked and then picked a bunch of flowers out of the infield and put them in his hand. Then they sat back and waited until dawn, when they knew the boys would be bringing the horses out to exercise them.

As the boys rode the horses onto the track, they pointed to Gary propped up in the middle of the track and yelled, "Go around him!" Gary was out cold. In fact, they'd dropped him as they were carrying him out to the track and had to roll him back on the stretcher, and he still hadn't woken up.

So anyway, these guys were coming along with their horses, and if you've ever stood beside a racetrack and watched the horses run by, it feels like the earth is moving, you know? And of course being a real hot dry day, there was a good cloud of dust behind each horse. So, they were just zooming by him, and finally Gary woke up. Two horses were coming right at him, one on each side, and they went thundering by him. He just kept looking straight ahead. Then he looked down at his flowers, then looked behind at the horses running off, then back at his flowers . . . and went back to sleep. After about four or five more horses thundered by him, I guess he finally realized what was going on. He stood up, picked up the cot, took his flowers, walked off the track and went straight back to his tent, and we didn't see him for the rest of the day.

But the memory I'm proudest of from those days was the time I made history as the first Governor General's Horse Guard to do an escort with an RCMP officer. It happened at the opening of an equestrian trail, an event scheduled to take place at the end of a 200-mile relay that I had ridden in as a Horse Guard.

I had been approached by a woman, Mavis McCullough, who had been working very hard to get the land and right of way to make this 200-mile trail. The trail, which was to be called the Great Pine Ridge Trail, was to be strictly equestrian; that is, exclusively for the use of activities connected to horses, whether it be riding or pulling wagons. Some of the land had been donated by the government, some by farmers. She had even gained permission to tunnel under busy highways. The ride I was to take was part of a deal she'd made with the government—if she would organize an inaugural ride, she got the land.

The ride was planned to take place over four days. Mavis had organized people to be on horses, pony carts, donkeys—anything equine—and to line up at various stops along the trail. It was my task to ride the entire length of the trail carrying a logbook and to get their signatures in this book.

In the four days it took to complete the ride, I met many people. Some would ride with me for a bit; some rode with me the whole day, covering 80 kilometres. At the end of their ride, they'd get picked up and taken back home again.

A park in Palgrave, Ontario was the scheduled destination. We all met again at a designated spot about eight kilometres before the end of the ride. The plan was to have masses of people on horses and on horse-drawn wagons all ride into the park together. I would be leading them in my capacity as a Governor General's Horse Guard along with an RCMP officer on horseback. It would be the first time ever that a Horse Guard and an RCMP officer did a side-by-side escort. I've lost the photograph but I'm told that when it happened—when the two of us came down over those rolling hills leading hundreds of people on every size, breed, colour of horse or horse-drawn mode of transportation—it was a phenomenal sight. You can imagine it meant a lot to me.

You know I'm not a believer in past lives or anything like that, but there was an occasion when we were doing the Queen's Plate race and we were escorting the Queen and Prince Philip. They had just climbed into the Landau. We took our formations and came around on the turf. It was dead quiet; all you could hear was the jingling of the harnesses on the horses. I was in a leading position riding at the corner of the formation with my sword out of its scabbard . . . and I had a déjà vu experience. I felt like a knight in armour going to battle. It was very a proud moment.

15 Closing the Door

I cherish those years, living with Sylvia and the kids and being in the Horse Guards. On a personal level, my life was rich. Even my parents—who had been among those who thought I was nuts to take on this large family—came to love Sylvia and understand why I was happy. Sylvia and I shared a lot. She even volunteered with the Horse Guards, working at their clubhouse. We were both committed to raising awareness of the best practices in equine care, and we took advantage of opportunities to do this with adults and children.

We started up a 4-H Pony Club in Pickering, Ontario; one of the first—if not *the* first—in the province and perhaps in Canada. However, we weren't getting any support for our efforts from the 4-H clubs in the area. Their focuses were on farm animals like cows and sheep—animals that put food on the table. They didn't recognize horses as agricultural animals, so we were forced to rely on the 4-H clubs in the United States for support materials, booklets and such things that we could give to our students.

This all changed when I was asked to provide an escort for E.P. Taylor.

E.P. Taylor was one of the wealthiest men in Canada. He made money in many ways, but he made his big money by expanding the brewery he'd inherited into the world's largest brewing company: Canadian Breweries Limited.

Importantly—to me, anyway—he was a total horse nut.

Taylor bred thoroughbred racing horses. He's the man who owned Northern Dancer, one of the most famous racehorses in Canadian history. He was president of the Ontario Jockey Club for 20 years and his horses won 15 Queen's Plate races. In 1976, E.P. Taylor was inducted into the Canadian Horse Racing Hall of Fame.

He had this amazing place, Windfields Farm, located in an area now known as the North Quadrant of Toronto. It was huge. I think there were something like 30 buildings on this estate—you could drive block after block and still be on the estate. The horses were behind white fencing; the Angus cattle behind black fencing. There was a veterinarian clinic located right on the ground.

He also had one of the largest collections anywhere of books and films about horses. Given his prestige and involvement in the Queen's Plate, it's perhaps not surprising that the British royal family often stayed at Windfields when they visited Toronto.

So it is also not surprising that E.P. was asked if he would speak at the grand opening for a special equine science program that was to be offered at Humber College in Toronto. That was when I met him and he started helping us with our 4-H Pony Club.

I had been asked to provide an official Horse Guard escort for Taylor at the opening. The man heading up the program had met me before when I had taken a course in animal husbandry that he'd been teaching at the University of Guelph. He knew I was with the Guards, so he called and asked if I could escort Taylor wearing the official Guards uniform. I checked with the Guards and they said, "Sure, you can do it." The GGHGs wouldn't normally provide an escort for an occasion like this, but of course E.P. Taylor was not an ordinary man, and the program was about horses and so had direct relevance for the Guards.

On the day in question, I had the occasion to talk with Taylor, and in the course of the conversation I told him about the 4-H Pony Club that Sylvia and I had started. I told him about the resistance we'd met from local 4-H clubs. He was surprised. He said, "Look, anything you need—*anything*—you just phone up the office and tell them who you are and what you're doing and they'll help you out."

He was true to his word. He sent films about horses over to us, and we would have film nights where our members could learn more about horses; all breeds, not just thoroughbreds. He'd arrange for guest speakers for our group. One time he arranged a special panel for us that included a trainer for the Canadian Olympic equestrian team, a member of the Canadian Olympic equine jumping team, one of Canada's top jockeys, and the vet from his own clinic. We had people attend that panel from throughout the equestrian community. It was a privilege to be able to put questions to those experts.

Once we started getting E.P. Taylor's support for our 4-H Pony Club, all of a sudden the other 4-H clubs started thinking maybe it was a viable thing and started supporting us, too. 4-H Pony Clubs began to form across the country.

The other great spin-off from that event was that I wangled my way into the equine science program. I wanted to take one of the night courses, but it was full. I spoke to Dick, the director, and he managed to get me in. It was a great course, my horse course.

I was learning about horses at the college and learning about life at home from Sylvia. She taught me so much. I mean, I was her husband and I was parenting the kids to some degree, but basically I was a young dude in a relationship with a woman. She had way more life experience than me, and thankfully, she was willing to share her knowledge. Sylvia helped me mature in terms of my awareness and attitudes toward women and their lot in life. She taught me things I'd never even thought about before, like what was really involved in childbearing and child rearing. I'd been married before and I had two kids of my own, but you know, I have to admit I wasn't the best husband or father then. I was still so much into my animals and partying. I was one of those guys who expected that my wife should look after the kids and the house and then look good for me. Even when Sylvia was trying to help me learn, I don't think I really took it all in. I don't think I had matured at all. Life was just day-by-day for me, and I never gave it a lot of thought. Sylvia set me straight on a lot of issues, but it wasn't until later in my life that when something happened when I was with a woman I'd start to think, "Oh, right, Sylvia used to talk to me about this."

So why did it all have to end? Well, basically, because while my personal life was rich, my financial life was in the dumps, and I felt like my career was going nowhere. The job working as a graphic artist with the Cash Register company had only lasted another six months and I'd been laid off again. Then I got a job driving for Dial-a-Bus in Pickering, a transportation service connected with the local GO Transit train. Dial-a-Bus was a good service. We'd pick people up at their houses and take them to the GO train, and then we also transported people from the GO train to other places and back in between GO train arrivals and departures.

But while the job itself was kind of fun, no matter how much money I made my pockets were always turned inside out. The kids always needed something and it was expensive to run the farm. We had 27 Morgan horses at that time. It just drained me financially and frustrated me mentally.

Sylvia could see my frustration and she sympathized. She thought Gord, her ex-husband, should have been helping more financially. Who knows what he did with his money, but he certainly wasn't using it to help his family. I think he might have been paying off a lot of his own debt.

Anyway, Sylvia thought it was too much responsibility for someone as young as I was, and she also thought that maybe if I wasn't around, he'd be forced to be a better provider for his kids. I wanted to get out from under the pressure, but I felt guilty and I cared about her and the kids. Ultimately, we agreed that it was time for me to move on and, just as the Captain of the Horse Guards had performed our marriage, he annulled it as well.

I knew I had to get away from the area, that I had to do something different. I decided to go west. I filled some shopping bags with clothes, grabbed my dog, put my hat on, went out to the 401 and stuck my thumb out. By that time my parents had moved to Vancouver, so that was a potential destination, but I really wasn't sure where I was going to end up or how long it would take me to get there. I thought if I had to work part-time jobs here and there to survive, I'd do that. The only thing I was sure of was that wherever I ended up, it would be something different. It would be an adventure. Four and a half days later, I ended up in Vancouver.

16 Moving On

It took 27 rides in 27 different cars to get to Vancouver. I met all kinds of people and had lots of different experiences on the road. The best rides were the transport trucks. Drivers would pick me up and take me long distances. The worst ride was one that turned out to be in a stolen car and scared the pants off me.

I wasn't out of Ontario yet when this young guy picked me up. There were two other young guys—teenagers—in the back who were also hitch-hiking. We got to a gas station in Sudbury and the guy driving got out to get gas, but he didn't turn off the motor. That should have been my first clue. When he got back in the car, he asked if I could drive so he could get some rest. I drove until we needed gas again, and then I pulled into a service station and stopped the car. When I went to turn the car off, I found there was no key, just some wires. I said to the guy, "What's this about?" He told me the car was his dad's and that his dad had the key at work. He said he'd received a call that his sister, who lived in Alberta, was dying and he'd had to leave so quickly he hadn't had time to get the key from his dad. Sketchy story, I know, but I was still thinking maybe he was telling the truth. So we drove a long way together, the four of us, with the three of us hitch-hikers paying for the gas.

When we reached Alberta, the guy asked if we wanted to drive with him to BC. I said, "How can you go to BC? Don't you have to see about your sister?" He said, "Well, I don't know what hospital she's in so there's no point." Okay, that's wrong. We got to Calgary and stopped at a McDonald's. The guy went in and I turned to the two guys in the back seat and said, "Look, there's no sister and I'm pretty certain this is a stolen car. I'm not going any further with this guy. What do you guys want to do?" They told me they were just going to go to a youth hostel in town, and they got out and left. When the guy came back to the car, I told him the other guys had gone to the youth hostel and suggested we go there, too. He climbed in, and once again fell asleep. I drove to the police station and parked the car in the chief's parking spot. Then I got out and left. I have no idea if they found him, but I've always imagined a scene in which the chief drives in and finds this guy in his spot. Need I say more?

The rest of the rides I had were pretty uneventful, but the rides stopped at Vancouver.

I fell in love with Vancouver. Instantly. I thought, "Wow. What a great place." My parents were surprised to see me. I hadn't known for sure I'd end up in Vancouver, so I hadn't told them I was coming, but fortunately, they were also glad to see me and welcomed me with open arms. Their concern, like mine, was with what to do next.

They suggested I go back to school, and I thought that was a great idea. I was 28 and I didn't know anybody in BC except Mom and Dad. I thought going to school would be a great way to meet people, especially girls. Mom and Dad were both in the art supply business—my dad did sales and my mom had an art supply store—and they knew I had some skills in that area, so they suggested I study art. Mom knew all the art teachers at Capilano College on the north shore, so she spoke to them on my behalf and they squeezed me in. Frankly, I'm not sure I deserved the special treatment. I liked doing art, but it wasn't a big deal for me. Like I said, I just went there because I wanted to meet people and have fun doing it.

I think this soon became clear to my instructors. For one thing, everything I did—no matter whether it was a drawing, painting, or a sculpture—was animal-related. Like, there would be a model up on the pedestal for sculpting class, and I'd end up sculpting a horse's head. I never put much detail in what I was doing, so the instructors often had no idea what any of it was.

The day I was building the horse's head, the teacher walked

by, and when he got to me he looked at what I was doing, and then he stopped and looked again real hard. Then he said, "What part of the body are you doing, Gary? It kind of looks like a horse's head to me." I had to admit it was. He said, "Well, I can't grade you on this. I mean, what's that got to do with what you're supposed to be doing?" I said, "It's okay, don't worry about it. Don't give me a grade." But he did.

Same thing would happen with life drawing. There would be a nude model up at the front. She (or he) would take a pose and I'd look and think, "Hmmmm. What animal does that remind me of?" and then I'd start drawing the model, adding parts of that animal to the model, like one I did of a female model where she ended up with a dog's head and six teats. Actually, a lot of people liked that one . . . including the model, who asked me to redraw it for her. It got so that after the sessions, everybody would come over and see what kind of creature I'd created.

The teacher finally gave up on me, but in the end he gave me top marks for my work. He said, "You know what? I've got to admire you. You stuck to your guns and ended up getting everyone interested in what you produced. You stepped out on a limb and that was good." He encouraged me to go further with my approach and suggested reference material, but art wasn't really my thing. I enjoyed it, and I still enjoy it once in a while, but it's always been something I felt I could do if there were no other options. I am thankful for his patience and open mind, though, because it must have been very frustrating for him and for the other teachers.

Actually, I became very good friends with my art history teacher, Ed Cotter.

Ed was a big teddy-bear kind of guy, really nice, but he always seemed to pick on me in class. I would question a particular approach or assumption and he would always push me hard about my argument. It seemed like he and I were always getting into debates in class. Sometimes it seemed like the rest of the class might as well go home, because we'd just be going at it. After the class, he'd come up to me, put his arm around my shoulder, and says "So. Meet me down in the coach house for a beer?" I didn't drink, but I'd go.

One day I asked him why he argued with me so much in class. He told me that it was because I spoke up the most, and that through our arguments, he thought the class was getting both sides of the issue. "Between the two of us, we're teaching them a lot." We became really good friends after that.

Then, on school break, he and his girlfriend Cathy went on a holiday; to Arizona, I think. They were driving and it was a really hot day and they had no air conditioning in the car. They decided to stop at a lake and cool down in the water. He stripped down, jumped in, and then surfaced and waved to Cathy. Then he went down and never came up again. Turns out he wasn't really waving at Cathy, he was trying to let her know something was wrong. They figure he had a heart attack, because he'd been so hot and then had jumped into the freezing cold water. It was too much of a shock for his system. It was a really sad moment, you know?

Anyway, I did graduate from that program, but it really didn't matter to me if I graduated or not. I was more interested in life outside of school, and much of my attention was focused on the new girls I was meeting and the jobs I got while I was going to school.

One of the first jobs I got was working at Sewell's Marina in Horseshoe Bay, West Vancouver. I needed the money and the place was pretty cool, so when they asked if I knew how to drive the big yachts anchored there, I said, "Oh, yeah." I'd never handled one in my life, but I thought it would be fun. I'd been on a big boat with my rich cousin Doug and had watched him work the throttles and the gears. I thought it couldn't be too hard. And it wasn't! Mostly I just delivered boats to people, pulling them on the back of a trailer.

The big test came one day when the foreman told me I had to take a cruiser over to a marina in Nanaimo. I went, "Oh, okay. So, when is it going to be pulled out of the water?" He said, "No, you're not driving this one. You're going to take it across the water to Nanaimo." He told me that all I had to do was head to the ferry terminal in Nanaimo, take a left, go down the shore for about a kilometre and a half and I'd see the marina right there. He, of course, did not know that I'd never been on the ocean in my life, let alone managed a big cruiser.

I'm thinking, "How the heck am I going to get out of this one?" I don't even know how to start the thing, and I have no idea how to get to the ferry dock in Nanaimo. On top of everything, it's a really crummy rainy day.

So I go down to the dock and climb aboard the cruiser and look it over, trying to figure out how to start it and everything.

When I climb back onto the dock, one of the mechanics is there and I say, "Hey, can you start this thing up and warm it up a bit for me? I've got to go to the bathroom really bad." He says, "Yeah, no problem, Gary."

By the time I come back, the boat's running and I have a plan. Sewell's Marina is located right by the ferry dock in Horseshoe Bay. I know the ferry is about to leave for Nanaimo, so I figure I'll drive the boat around the point where they can't see me and then I'll just hover there in neutral until the ferry leaves. Then I'll just pull in behind it and follow it all the way to Nanaimo. When it gets to the terminal, I'll head left to the marina.

So I get in the boat, and I'm about ready to put it in gear, when I hear this guy yelling at me. I stick my head out and say, "What?" He says, "I've got to untie you first." I go, "Of course, I know that. I was just revving it up." He looks at me kind of weird but unties the boat, and then I back out. I know where reverse is. I manage to turn it around, and then I go very slowly around the point. The ferry pulls out just on cue, and I follow it. At one point we hit a bit of fog and I can't see the ferry. I think, "Oh my God. I'm probably going to end up in Japan." But finally, I see it again and pull in behind.

We got to Nanaimo and I turned left, as instructed, and found the marina no problem. There was a guy there out on the end of the dock waving at me to pull into this empty slip in between two other boats. I thought, "There's no way I am going to try to do this." There was an empty dock near the end of the marina so I managed to get the boat in there. The guy ran over and grabbed the front of the boat and started tying me up. Me? I just wanted off. I left the boat running and in neutral, climbed out, and said to the guy, "Listen, I want to see if I can get that ferry back. Is there anybody here that can drive me to the ferry while you take care of this boat?" He said, "No problem, just go up to the office and they'll drive you back."

Fortunately, they never asked me to do that again, and I only really screwed up big enough that they could notice it one more time. That was the time I accidentally kicked the box of tools off the dock and into the water.

Garth, my boss, told me I'd have to go and get the tools. I said, "How deep is it?" He said, "About 20 feet." I said, "I can't go down that deep," plus the water was really cold. Garth told me there was a wetsuit, tank and mask in the boathouse I could use. I told him I couldn't scuba dive. He said, "Well, maybe it's time you learn." So, I never retrieved the tools—someone else did that—but I did learn to scuba dive.

Garth sent me to a place called the Diving Locker where he knew this guy, Ian. He said, "Tell Ian I sent you and he'll give you a good price on diving lessons." I was like, "Yes!" I was pretty excited about taking diving lessons.

Thing was, I was really a weak swimmer. I just didn't have the stamina for any kind of distance swimming, and in order to get lessons for scuba diving you had to be able to swim. They made us swim many lengths of the pool. Everyone else finished way ahead of me; I still had two more lengths to do when they had finished, but I managed to do it. Then we had to hold our breath, and I aced that, but then we had to play volleyball while treading water the whole time. I could not do that. Well . . . I did it for maybe 30 seconds, but then I just held my breath and went under. I kept treading water and kept my hands above the surface. I felt the volleyball hit my hands a few times, but I couldn't keep my body above the water. I was sure they weren't going to pass me, but they did. I puked my guts out, I was so sick from doing that. But they passed me, and so I thought, "Great!" I was so excited.

Learning to scuba dive was a different matter. With the equipment on, and being underwater, I was in my element. Everything worked and I felt good. I could hardly wait to get out to the ocean and dive. I bought some really good gear and I did a lot of diving. However, when I got a chance to work with horses again, I went for it.

I'd met a woman at the college who said she was keeping a horse at the Corral Riding Academy, located right across the street from the college. She told me that the horse was just a bit over two years old, but unbroken. She knew I'd worked with horses and asked if I could help with the training. I told her I'd train the horse and then train her with her horse. So that's what I did. I'd go up there and spend an hour each day before I went to work. Eventually I got the horse broken, and then taught her how to ride it. The people at the Corral recognized that I could train and had a lot of riding experience, so they offered me a job teaching riding lessons and breaking horses.

I was back with horses and loving it.

It was through giving riding lessons that I met and started dating Nadine. Nadine owned a half-Arabian colt. One day she came to me and said, "Would you be interested in buying an Arabian colt?" I said, "How much is it?" She said, "Oh, I don't know, somewhere around $20,000." I told her I didn't have that kind of money, so she said, "Well, I've got some money, and if you can come up with some, then we could pay it off later. The guy is willing to do that."

The horse's name was Sarazin; a beautiful bay with a silver mane and tail. We bought it, but it meant I had to sell all my scuba gear, and I was *still* short of my share. I needed to make more money than I could get working part-time at the Corral.

As things would happen, a few days later I was at my mom's art supply store and this guy, Richard, came in. Mom knew him from the time when he had been an art supply salesman. Richard was starting up a new business producing picture frames. He showed Mom these metal picture frames he said he'd gotten in California and asked what she thought of them. She told him they were great frames. He said, "Yeah, I've been getting that response wherever I go." Then he explained that he'd opened up a little shop to produce the frames, but he needed someone to manage it for him so he could be out making the sales. Mom said, "Well, Gary's not working now. Maybe he can do it for you." I looked at the frames and thought they were pretty cool, that I could get into making them, and so he hired me.

The shop was really an unfinished basement in a commercial building, and my job was to measure and chop the metal, and put the mats together with the frames. Richard said he would help me, but I was pretty much on my own. I filled the orders and delivered them and otherwise ran the place. He only came in a couple of times to show me the process, and then he'd leave. I thought, "This is weird. This isn't going to go anywhere."

Next thing I know, two plainclothes cops show up at my door, except I don't know that's what they are at first. They say, "Who are you?" I say, "My name's Gary Oliver." He says, "Okay." I say, "Who are you?" So they flash their badges. I say, "What's this about?" and they say they're looking for Richard, do I know him?

"Yeah, I do."

"When was the last time you saw him?"

"Two weeks ago, maybe?"

"Whose business is this?"

"It's his, but he wanted me to be a partner in it."

"So you haven't seen him for two weeks? Have you opened up your mail?"

"I don't get any mail."

"Is any of the mail that's come here addressed to you?"

"You know what? I don't know. I've never even looked at it. I just pick it up and put it in the pile."

"Do you mind looking at it? See if there's something addressed to you."

So, I'm looking through it, and sure enough there's an envelope there addressed to me. They say, "Do you want to open it, please?" So I open it, and he says, "Read it, and then if you don't mind, we'd like to see it." I'm thinking, "This is really weird."

So I read it. It's a letter from Richard informing me that by the time I open the letter, he'll be dead, that he's committing suicide. He wrote "I've gotten way over my head in things—debts, problems with my wife, my girlfriend, everything. I can't deal with this anymore, Gary, the company is yours."

I was stunned.

Then they read it. I said, "Has he committed suicide?" They said, "Well, we found his car on the ferry and we found his jacket floating in the water with some of his ID, so we're assuming right now that that's a possibility, but until we find a body we can't really say for sure. If you hear anything from Richard, let us know. You might also want to let any people that are dealing with his business know that he is no longer in business."

I noticed when I was going through the mail that there were a lot of letters from the bank, so the bank was one of the places I told. I showed them a copy of the letter. They said, "Are you a partner in the company?" I said, "No, not officially. There's nothing written down, but I know he wanted me to be a partner."

That night, I was thinking about all that and got an idea. I realized that I had a lot of contacts in the art world, both through school and from when I used to travel with Dad when he was selling art supplies. He would ask me if I wanted to tag along when he had to travel to places in BC or out-of-province. It was a great way for me to see the area, so if I'd had a school break or felt I could miss some time, I'd go with him. I was already getting a favourable response to this product from local clients; I figured it'd sell elsewhere, too.

I went back to the bank and made a pitch. I told them that I'd come up with an idea: to put them in packages of different lengths. Then people could buy the length they wanted and build their own frames. They went, "Yeah, that's a good idea."

I said, "Yeah, and I could get the packaging made." They said, "Well, what do you want to invest in this?" I went, "Invest?" I was living off employment insurance benefits, right? I said, "Well, I was thinking that I could take over the assets of the company, then build on the contacts I have, like . . . my mom owns an art supply store, and I know all these people, and I know I could sell this product."

They said, "Okay. All right," and then we talked about what would be involved in me doing this. They said I'd have to get a new name, because I couldn't go by Super Graphic, the current company name. I thought about it and came up with the name "Eagle Frames," because I like eagles. They liked that name and told me that I'd need to get it registered, and that I'd need a lawyer. I said, "Well, gee, I don't have the money for that until I sell some of the products." He said, "Bring me back some information about yourself and give me your mother's phone number right now. I'm going to phone her." Mom told him, "Yeah, Gary's not lying. He does know a lot of people in this industry through travelling with his dad, you know?" So, they said, "Okay, we'll give you $50,000 in a rotating loan. You get your lawyer, get your name registered and get the business going." Eagle Frames was born, and I had 50 grand in my pocket (so to speak).

And I was right: it was a really successful company. It made money hand over fist, an unbelievable amount. I got contracts with Eaton's, and Woodward's, and Sears, and the Bay, and I was selling to framing companies from here to Saskatchewan. I made new clients on my own, but I also sold to many of those who had known my dad and were willing to deal with me based on that alone.

I was rolling in dough. I had 12 people just chopping frames and I had rented a bigger place. It was pretty amazing. I was getting close to being a millionaire through that little venture. But I'm getting ahead of myself.

Having that $50,000 also meant I could throw a few thousand dollars in to pay off the horse. And then a friend of Nadine's who had a farm out in Aldergrove (in the Fraser Valley, outside of Vancouver) had to go out of the country for five years and needed someone to live in the house. The rent would be real cheap; basically just managing the farm. It was a pretty little place, had a pond and the whole works. He'd just finished building a brand new bar and putting in fencing. It was also right next door to a riding academy with 72 stalls.

By that time, Nadine and I were an established couple. We

decided to take the place together and start breeding Arabian horses. We called the farm "Hy-Az-A-Kyte Arabians." Another door had opened.

17 Living Hy-Az-A-Kyte

We called our farm Hy-Az-A-Kyte because when people talk about Arabian horses, they describe them as being high as a kite. Arabians are thought to be hot-blooded, a bit crazy. I always said they're not crazy, they're just more perceptive than any other breed. You know, when they see a leaf, they react to it. An Appaloosa just sort of goes, "Duh, what's up?"

But we were also living high as a kite.

We began breeding Arabians, starting with breeding the horse I bought with Nadine's horse, Dancer. We bought a few, too—well, mostly Nadine was buying horses. I was still running the framing business. I'd come home from work and there'd be a horse in the barn and I'd go, "Whose horse is this?" And she'd say, "Ours."

"Where did we get it?"

"Well, Quilchena Arabian out in New Westminster had a filly sale. I went there and I saw this one. They gave me a really good deal on her. She's ours."

"What was the good deal?"

"Well, we got her for $22,000. She was cheap."

She was spending my money as fast as I was making it.

In the end we had 32 Arabian horses and we were getting quite a name in the Arabian horse world as breeders.

We had a pretty good life. Did I mention that Nadine was a knockout? Oh, yeah. She was like a model: Beautiful, young—11 years younger than me—sea-blue eyes with bright red hair. She was a girl who could sweep any man off his feet.

And I wasn't that bad, either.

Actually, one of the stories that sticks most in my mind from those days involves an impression of me as a lady killer. And believe me, I hadn't done anything to deserve it.

It was in August. It was really hot and hadn't rained for a few days and we were out of water. We got our water from a well—so it was groundwater—and the valley was dry. We phoned a water supply company and they said they were backlogged with orders to fill people's wells because everyone was dry. They said they'd send someone out, but he might not get there till midnight. We said that was no problem.

The guy didn't get there until 11:30 that night. He put the hose down in the well and turned on the water. Just then, Nadine came walking out of the house in her babydoll nightie. I took one look at her and then walked over to her and said, "What the heck are you doing, coming out here like that?" She says, "Well, it's hot!" I said, "Yeah, I know!" but suggested she go back in and told her I'd be in as soon as we finished. She went, "Yeah, okay," but then just stood there.

Well, we happened to have seven young girls staying in our bunkhouse at the farm just then because they wanted to work with horses. Some of them had horses boarded at the stable next door. I guess this night they were all in the house with Nadine and cooked up this plan to embarrass me. Anyway, the next thing I knew, one of them came out also dressed in her babydoll pyjamas. And then one by one the rest of them came out like that.

The guy who was pumping the well was just looking at all these women and he said, "Can I talk to you?" I said, "Yeah, sure."

We walked around the other side of the truck and he said, "What kind of a place do you have here?" I said, "It's a horse stable. Why?" He said, "Well, I noticed the sign, Hy-Az-A-Kyte Arabian Stud Services. Tell me, who's the stud?"

It soon became obvious that after he left, he shared this story with others: about a week later, I got a call from the Arabian Horse Association. They were having a stallion show at the Thunderbird Equestrian Show Park, an event where anybody with stallions could show up, show their breed, and promote their stallion. The Association wanted to do a bit of a pageant and wanted to know if I would be willing to dress up as a sheikh. There would be women fanning me while horses would be paraded by in front of me as if I were a big time Arabian horse buyer. I said, "Yeah sure, I can do that."

My mom made me a great sheikh costume, and I also had a stuffed hawk that I would be holding in one hand. A fellow from the local Aldergrove Star newspaper came out and took photos of me to promote the Arabian stallion exhibition. He took several photos of me all dressed up with the hawk in one hand and the halter rope of one of my Arabian stallions in the other.

A couple of days later there I am in the Aldergrove Star. There were two or three photos with one big one of me with the horse and the hawk. The caption read: "Gary Oliver, his Arabian horses, and his harem will be at the Thunderbird Equestrian Show Park for the Arabian Stallion Exhibition." I couldn't believe it: the story actually made the papers.

The farm was great and Nadine and I got along well until things began going downhill with the framing business. Other framing companies had started bringing in their own metal picture frames and they were buying them in Mexico for half the price that I was paying for the ones I was bringing in from California. On top of that, this was the late '70s and there was a downturn in the economy. When times are bad, luxury items are the first to go. By 1979, my business had dropped off the map. I went from making hundreds of thousands of dollars to maybe single-digit thousands. I could barely pay my rent for the office and I had to let my staff go. Finally, I just couldn't do it anymore. I shut down the framing business.

Truth be told, my heart wasn't really in it. I sort of fell into this company and everything was handed to me—the bank had been willing to give me money, the products were there, the customers were there, the desire to have the products was there. It was too good to pass up. It was exciting while it lasted, but my heart wasn't in it. I had faith I could find something else.

In the meantime, though, I had to do something about money. We'd used up all the money buying horses so I still owed the bank $50,000 and we had the farm to run.

I managed to sell off the company's assets and that gave me a bit of money to survive on, but not much more. I went back to judging horse shows just to make a bit of side money until I could figure out how to keep the farm, because the framing business had been largely supporting the horse operation. One thing was sure: we couldn't afford to keep buying up horses and not selling them.

I told Nadine we had to sell some of the horses. We'd had ten foals born that year, so I said, "Let's sell some of the babies. We don't need this many horses and we can make some money." One of our horses had come in the top ten in the Arabian nationals. We'd been given an offer of $50,000 right there on the spot for him and we'd turned it down. I said, "Maybe he'll take it now. We could sell to that guy and get some money to hold us over until I can get something going again."

But she wouldn't. Nadine did not want to sell any of the horses. We argued back and forth about this a lot.

Finally, the bank started putting pressure on me. I talked to my friend who was a business consultant to get some advice from him. He told me that I could either declare bankruptcy, in which case I'd lose everything—the farm, the horses, everything—or, he said, I could just walk away from the company, remain unemployed, and refuse to pay anything. I said, "Well, what about my assets?" He said I'd have to get rid of them or they would be taken, that I should make sure they were not in my name.

So I put them in Nadine's name, everything. We were engaged, officially—it was even written in the papers—so it seemed the obvious thing to do. Then I had to leave town for three days to judge a horse show in Alberta.

When I came back, everything was gone; everything, except my dog and some show saddles I'd won bull-riding, plus my clothes and a few books. Everything else—the horses, the horse saddles, the trailers—everything had vanished.

I had no idea where Nadine had gone, so for the next several days I cruised around the area looking for my horses. It's all country out there and I figured I might see them out in a field.

Finally somebody said, "Hey, you know what? I think I saw your horses down on 6th Avenue, just east of 200th." I said, "Really?" So away I went, and sure enough there were my horses.

I pulled into the driveway and couldn't help noticing the brand new Corvette in the driveway. Nadine came out of the house.

I said to her, "What's going on?"

"What do you think is going on?"

"Well, you tell me."

"I left you."

"Yeah, well, you know, 50 percent of this stuff is mine. Except for the Corvette, where did you get that?"

"Let's say it's a gift."

"Well, 50 percent of everything else is mine."

To which she said, "It's all in my name. You're going to have a hard time getting it. You'll have to take me to court for it. And you know what? If you take me to court and you do get it, I'll just report you to the bank, and they'll just take it away from you as assets. So you'll be spending money on court fees to get nothing."

The next thing I know, out walked my insurance salesman. I put two and two together: Nadine had left me for him, and he'd left his wife and kids and home to be with her.

I said, "So *that's* who bought you the Corvette." She didn't say anything. I just looked at him and said, "She got me for everything. Good luck." And I walked away, and that was the last time I saw her. That was it. I closed that door for good.

All in all, I wasn't sad about losing the framing business, and I sure wasn't sad about losing Nadine, but I was very sad about losing the horses.

And of course, I now had absolutely nothing.

I was too proud to go to my parents or my friends and tell them that I'd lost everything. I couldn't ask for help and I didn't know what to do, so I went down to the east side of Vancouver where I knew I could get a free meal and maybe find a bed to crash in for the night. I ended up staying six months.

18 On the Street

Vancouver's Downtown Eastside is widely known as a devastated community populated by the most marginalized individuals society has to offer, from crack-addicted street workers (and the men who make their money off them) to lost souls whose minds went somewhere else long ago. It's much worse today than it was when I lived there almost 30 years ago, but even then it was home to the poorest of the poor.

I was one of them while I was there. I was one of those standing in line for food at the missions and I made use of the services for street people offered at Carnegie Hall. Most nights I was able to get a bed in an overnight shelter, but there were several nights I slept in the local park. It wasn't a comfortable life, but I figured it was temporary. This was a side of life I'd never experienced. For the people living it, it was depressing; for me, it was fascinating. And I had an advantage—I was not addicted to alcohol or drugs like most of the other people on the street. And unlike so many I met who had no sense of themselves as worthwhile, and who felt powerless, I felt pretty strong. I was bummed out about what Nadine had done, but otherwise I felt pretty good about myself. And, if worst came to worst, I could ask my parents for help. I just didn't want to do that. I knew I could find work, but I didn't want to go take a job for the sake of having a job, so I figured I'd make do while I sorted myself out. Was it time to stick my thumb out and try a new city, or what? I didn't know. At the same time, I was learning that I certainly didn't want to spend too long living on the streets. It was a humbling experience.

*　*　*

One of the things I've learned in life—and I think of my grandfather often at these times—is that you never know which lesser door is going to lead to a main door. I would never have imagined that a conversation with a Hare Krishna would lead to a door that would take me in an entirely new and exciting direction in my life.

I was sitting in the park and one of them came and sat beside me. He said, "You don't look like you belong here." I said, "Why? What makes you think that?"

"You just don't have that look about you. Do you drink or do drugs or anything?"

"No, not at all."

"Do you have any kind of criminal record?"

"None whatsoever."

"Then you really don't belong here, do you?"

"No, I don't, but I'm here right now."

So then he asked what I was doing there and I told him a bit of my story. He said, "If you ever need food, anytime, we have a little storefront just a few blocks away that we've made into our temple. If you just go down there and just tell them I referred you, they'll give you a meal. All healthy stuff, mind you, but it'll fill your belly. You can come down anytime and feel free to ask for help."

I went down once and they gave me this great big meal, more than I could eat. They were really nice. They didn't try to get me to shave my head or try to convert me, or anything. They were just . . . nice, you know?

The next time I decided to walk down there, fate hit and my whole life changed again.

I was on my way to their storefront temple. I had to go to the bathroom really bad and I had just started down West Pender Street between Hamilton and Homer when there was this building. The front door was open, so I thought, "Right. There has to be a bathroom here I can use."

I go up to the second floor and I'm looking around for the bathroom when I notice these two French doors, all glass, with a "For Rent" sign on them. I'm curious, so I walk over and look through the door. There's this huge auditorium. It's in bad shape, very dirty, but it's got hardwood floors and it's totally bare.

Just at that point, someone tapped me on the shoulder and I turned around and they said, "Can I help you?" To save face, I said, "Yeah, I'm interested in this hall. I see it's for rent." He said, "That's right." He told me he was the caretaker and that the place used to be a dance hall, but he said if I was thinking of it for that, I should know that fire regulations had changed and it couldn't be used for that anymore. I said I hadn't been thinking of it for a dance hall.

So he opens the door in the meantime, we walk in, and it's this amazing place. It's got like 22-foot ceilings, and a mural that goes down the whole side of the wall. There's a stage at one end, and a balcony running down the side of the room. I think, "Wow, this is huge." It's as big as the Commodore, a major dance hall in Vancouver. He tells me it's called the Pender Auditorium and that it was built back in 1908.

I later learned more about the building, which had a really rich history. It had originally been owned by the Marine Workers and Boiler Makers Industrial Union, Local No.1, and the mural (done in 1947) was a historical painting of industrial activity on Vancouver's waterfront. The auditorium had been a labour meeting hall in its time, but eventually labour moved out and the auditorium became a dance hall known as the Afterthought. Some of the biggest rock groups of the '60s and '70s played at the Afterthought, including the Grateful Dead, and the hall got a reputation as a centre for Vancouver's countercultural scene. In previous times it had been a boxing arena and even a bowling alley. However, by the time I saw the auditorium, it had been vacant for years.

So he said, "What did you have in mind?" I said, "An art studio." This was really the first thing that came into my mind. He said, "It's kind of big for an art studio, isn't it?" I said, "Well, it will be a community art studio. I'll divide it up and rent it to artists." He thought that was a good idea. I said, "Yes, this is just the sort of space I've been looking for." Then I said, "Hey, you know what? Do you have a bathroom handy? I've really got to use the bathroom." He said, "Yeah, right across the hall." Then he said, "The landlord isn't usually here, but he's in the building right now. Maybe I can find him and you can talk to him about renting the space." I said, "Yeah, okay." So he went off to find the landlord and I went to the bathroom, all the time thinking I'd go and then get out quick before he got back with the landlord. I had no intention of renting that space. How could I?

Well, the landlord must have been in the next room, because by the time I came out of the bathroom he was already standing there. He said, "Bill here tells me that you're interested in the space." I went, "Yeah, well, I kind of am. It depends." He said, "Depends on what?" By that time we'd walked back into the auditorium. I said, "This place is filthy." He said, "Well, it hasn't been used for a few years." Clue one.

I said, "Well, here's my proposition. Give me two months free rent, and in that time I'll take care of cleaning up the space. I want to make this an art community, but I need to advertise. If I get enough tenants to fill it up, you've got yourself a tenant. If I don't, at least the place will be cleaner, and you've got a better opportunity to rent it to somebody." Not surprisingly, since he hadn't had any tenants for years, he thought that was a good arrangement. He said, "Okay. Go upstairs with Bill and give him an address and let him know where to get in touch with you." Of course I didn't have an address at the time, but I gave him a friend's address. They gave me the keys right then and there.

I went back into the space and I thought, "What am I going to do now?" I walked to the back where the stage was, and on the right-hand side of the stage was a room, and in that room was a ladder that led to a trap door in the ceiling. I climbed up and opened the trap door. There was this huge loft with windows overlooking the North Shore—you could see the water and mountains. It was a gorgeous view. I thought, "Okay. This is where I'm going to live." It was perfect. I was going to make it work.

Coincidentally, my mother's art supply store was in that block. I went down and I said, "Guess what? I'm moving in to the building." She went, "What?" I said, "Yeah, I'm moving into the building right next to you." Again she said, "What?" I guess she was a bit stunned. I said, "Yeah. Do you have any chalk?" She said, "Yes," and gave me some chalk. So I thanked her, took the chalk and a pad of paper and a pencil, and I went upstairs and I marked out squares to designate about thirty spaces for artists. Then I made a sign that said "Art studio spaces for rent. Come and view between 3:00pm and 8:00pm any day."

In the morning I would run around putting up those signs in art supply stores. I put one in Mom's store, and I put up signs in galleries, and in schools like the Emily Carr Institute of Art and

Design and Capilano College (where I had gone to school)—in any place I could think of where there might be artists. Within the month, I had every space rented.

You might wonder what possessed me to do that. Well, animals had been the biggest part of my life for a long time, but art had always been there in the background, and right then it seemed like art might be the route to a bit of money . . . and money was a pretty immediate need.

I charged everybody $100/month for rent, plus a $100 security deposit. By the end of the two months, I'd collected $6000. My own rent was $975 a month. I arranged for a phone. I cleaned up my space and got some furniture. I was ready for business.

I called it the "Pacific Artists Studio." I designed a little logo for it and everything. It was an incredible space, and it became an incredible community. I spent the next 12 years of my life managing the Pacific Artists Studio.

19 Pacific Artists Studio

Over 315 people rented space in the Studio over those years. At any one time there would be 30 or so. I had no problem filling the spaces; it was instant. I guess there was no place for artists to go, and the idea of a community where they would be able to bounce ideas off of fellow artists and borrow equipment and things like that had a strong appeal.

When an artist would come in for the first time, they'd say, "Where's the space?" I'd say, "Pick out a square and that's your space." They'd say, "What about walls? Like, where are my walls?" I'd say, "Make your own. I don't care how you do it. It's a community space, be creative."

In the beginning the walls were made of everything from canvas to wicker to wooden pallets—pretty much whatever they could find—and that's how it remained until after our first open house, when I got this very generous offer from one of the people who came to see the art.

Cosmos was this crazy Greek guy. He came up to me at the end of the show and introduced himself. He told me that he was the head of the model-building department of H.A. Simons Ltd., a company that built huge oil refineries. It was his job, he said, to produce small-scale models of the plans. Turns out they had a whole bunch of wall partitions stored in the company's basement that they were going to have to get rid of soon. He offered to donate them to the studio. I thanked him, but said I had no way to get them here, so he even offered to arrange for them to be brought over.

A few days later the partitions arrived. They were terrific. They stood about six feet high and were made of aluminum framing with drywall at the bottom and frosted glass on the top. Getting them up the stairs to the auditorium was a challenge, but Cosmos had sent a crew of men with the partitions, so while it was a struggle, we finally got them up and then I spent the next two weeks putting them up. When they were finally up, they made the place look great—much more professional. However, that didn't happen for a while, and until then we just had a crazy patchwork of spaces, which actually suited the crazy patchwork of artists that used them.

We had every kind of artist there—painters and sculptors, but also artists, and some who made costumes and trinkets. It was an incredible range. There were big-name people who visited the place like Tony Onley and Jack Shadbolt, but mostly the people who used the Pacific Artists Studio were your typical starving artists, although several became successful in later years.

There were people like Iain Baxter (a well-known artist and later an instructor at UBC), and Sam Black, another UBC instructor. Jack Darcus, who has a gallery in Vancouver to this day, is one of those who came through the Studio. One of the artists— I think her name was Jennifer—later painted a mural on the side of the Vancouver General Hospital that unfortunately got obliterated when a new section of the hospital was built. And there was Wendy Tosoff, who did water colours of teddy bears and clowns. Wendy's work got picked up by Hallmark Cards, so she was one of those who became quite successful. Same with Rita Stapleton (who's now a top-notch airbrush special effects artist working in the film industry), and John-Franco Avione, who did all the wax sculptures in the wax museum in Niagara Falls.

Many, many characters used the space at Pacific Artists Studio. There were even a few musicians who'd rent a space I had that was isolated from the others. Doug Bennett (of "Doug and the Slugs") rented that space for about two months to do some recording. He was a cool guy. I could see he had sort of an air about him, that he figured he was somebody special, but other than that he was okay. He was a good tenant.

Even the Royal Architectural Institute of Canada's BC chapter rented space from me for a while.

And, of course, there was Carol. Carol made belly dance costumes out of coin belts and coin bras. We became friends and she got me interested in belly dancing. I got to know most of the belly dancers in town and started going to some of the belly dancing jamborees at a local Greek club. The girls would always get me up to belly dance. I even took lessons from one of the girls, and later, when I was doing photography, I'd do photos of them for their portfolios.

Photography! That was another thing I kind of fell into.

The Pacific Artists Studio had been going for about three months when one of the tenants came up and said, "I can't pay my rent, I'm broke, but I have a Pentax camera. Would you consider taking that in lieu of rent?" I was feeling flush at the time, so I said, "Sure, okay."

So I put some film in it and started taking photos. At the time, I was dating this girl—a model that I'd met at our first open house—so I took some pictures of her. She took the roll of film and got it developed and then, because she was connected with the John Casablancas International Model Management, she showed them the photos. A woman from the Casablancas agency phoned me and said, "Hey, we really like those photos you did of Leslie. If we send you some models, could you do some more for us?" I said I could, but that we were right in the middle of renovations just then, and she said, "Well, okay. Give us a call when you're ready, because you do nice work." Truth is, I didn't know anything about photography, but it hit me that maybe I could become a fashion photographer. She also asked me if I had other samples of work that I'd done. I said, "Yeah, I've got a whole bunch of them, but they're in Toronto." I wasn't lying. In the old days I'd had a little Kodak Brownie that I used to take pictures of my dog and friends and things like that, but I didn't tell them that.

What I did was put an ad in the paper: "Photo Studio for Rent." I'd saved a good space for myself to do my own art, but I'd been too busy being a janitor for 30 artists to do any work of my own. However, I did need some kind of creative outlet, and thought photography might be it, especially as it could bring in some extra income. First, though, I had to learn how to do it. Fortunately, I had a plan.

Photographers started coming in. I'd show them the space and they'd ask what the rent was. I'd say, "It's free," to which they'd say, "What's the catch?" I would say, "Well, the catch is that I've been asked to do photography, but I don't have any equipment beyond a camera. I thought if you were interested, we could each book time in the space and in return for you using the space, I could use your lighting system. Most said no, because even if they were willing to share the space, with the walls being no higher than six feet it was too open for them.

Finally a fellow named John Morrison—a well-known photographer in the area—came in. He said, "You know what, this suits me perfectly. I have so much equipment and it's sitting in the middle of my living room. I don't have a studio, and I need a place to put this equipment. I'd probably only need to use the studio a couple of times a month because I do most of my work outside." I said, "Great. Oh, and one more thing: can you teach me how to use it?" He said, "I thought you were a photographer." I said, "No, I'm just learning, but I've got clients already and I've got to get this going, you know?" He said, "Sure. I can teach you in a day." And he did. He showed me how to set up the lights and tripod and all and he wrote right on the floor what things like the "F-stop" were about.

So I had a studio and equipment and a bit of knowledge. I called the modelling agency and they started sending over models. I ended up being quite successful. Word got around, and I ended up shooting for several agencies, including Blanche Macdonald's (when she was still alive). I got jobs working for the Westender newspaper, doing their fashion page. When I had to do something with which I was unfamiliar, I'd call up John and he'd tell me things like where to place the lights for that kind of shoot. I was lucky to have him and a couple of other photographers who also gave me that kind of help. One year I was chosen by Vancouver Magazine as one of the top ten fashion photographers in the city, which was pretty funny, but I really have to share that credit with those other guys.

About the same time that I started doing photography, I also started taking dance lessons. I'd always loved dancing, of course, but I'd never taken any formal lessons. There was an artist named Ken Wesman that I'd become friends with and Ken talked me into coming to some classes he was taking with a guy named Jack Ellard. Jack taught ballroom dancing, like Latin dancing, but he also taught break-dancing, dirty dancing, and what was known as street dancing—a kind of modern swing. I really enjoyed this stuff and it didn't take too long before Ellard could see that this kind of dancing was pretty natural for me. He ended up putting me on his formation team and getting me to help teach the classes. I ended up giving lessons in the evenings to other people who wanted to learn to dance. As usual, I took advantage of any opportunity to make some extra money, but my knowledge was still limited, so if they wanted to go beyond the beginner level, I had a deal with Jack that I'd send them on to him and in return, he gave me free lessons. All of that dancing came in real handy when we put on our fabulous Pacific Artists Studio open houses.

We all collaborated to plan and execute the open houses. They were major affairs—the biggest and best you've ever seen. All 30 of the artists would be displaying their work in their spaces and offering appetizers to those who came by. One of the artists' husbands was a guy named Catfish Willie who had a great three-piece slap-bass band, and they'd be playing. There was a terrific gay club downstairs and we'd take that over and put on fashion shows and magic shows, and various people—including me—would put on dance demonstrations. The gay guys would put on a drag show for everybody. It was hilarious.

These guys who ran the gay club were the best neighbours. I used to go down there every week to watch the drag shows, and we became friends. In fact, when they found out that I had no bathroom facilities up at my loft—the only bathroom was that one outside the auditorium in the hall, and so I had no place to shower or anything—they gave me a key to the baths they had in their place. I only used it between six and seven in the morning, and there was no one there then so it worked great. They had a nice big Jacuzzi and a gym and it was all brand new, they'd just built it.

So all in all we had a good community thing going. We even had a baseball team and we were part of a league. The league had players from companies like IBM and Air Canada and Nestlé. We were "the Starving Artists." We had uniforms and t-shirts and a hat with a picture of Babe Ruth on it or something. We never won anything, but we had a lot of fun.

There was only one guy I asked to leave. He was an Australian guy named Christian. He was a good artist, but he was abusive to the women at the PAS, really demeaning. And he was demeaning to the gay guys downstairs. He was very strange, and finally I asked him to leave. I didn't want to put up with that.

But mostly the people who came there were good people.

It was a tight community. We had a lot of fun in the studio, too. One guy, Dan Malick—a guy who'd come from Calgary and who painted funny little sayings on river rocks that he sold to novelty stores—used to go to flea markets and come back with gifts for everybody in the studio. Some of them even ended up getting married and have kids.

I have only one really sad memory from that time.

I'd started going out with this girl, Joanne. Everyone loved her, including my parents. She was just a really delightful young woman. We went to clubs and dinners and parties and she just fit right in comfortably with whomever we were with or wherever we were. We'd been going out for about four months, and she was pretty much living with me, when one day she went down to the store. While she was gone, I had to go up to the loft and her ID was on the bed. I was looking at the picture of her on the ID when I noticed the birth date. She was only sixteen! I thought she was 26. We all did. My heart dropped into my stomach and I thought, "Oh my God. I can't be going out with a 16-year-old girl."

When she came back, I confronted her about it. I said, "We have to do something. You should still be in school." She told me she'd left home because her mom had thrown her out after her sister found a marijuana joint in Joanne's dresser drawer. She and her mom had never got along and she felt she could not go back home. I called Social Services and asked if they could help her out. They said they could, that she could stay in a foster home.

She went through three foster homes. She dropped in to see me after the first and second foster homes. She said the man in the first foster home had been hitting on her; the couple in the second home were extremely religious and kept trying to convert her. She didn't come back to see me after she was placed in the third home. She just disappeared. I got very worried, because there were lots of things she had left at the studio that I knew she valued; things like her photograph albums, her scrapbooks and diaries. Social Services would give me no information, even when I said that I had all this stuff for her. I heard rumours that she was working the streets on Davie, an area frequented by sex-trade workers. I drove around looking for her, but I never found her.

Then one day, I'd been having dinner with my parents and they were driving me back to the studio. We were driving along Hastings and were about five or so blocks from the Studio when I saw Joanne standing on the sidewalk in front of a hotel. She looked horrible. My parents didn't see her, and I didn't tell them she was there because they would have been very upset at what had happened to her. About a block later, I said, "Dad, can you pull over? I'm feeling a bit nauseous. I'll just get out and walk the rest of the way." He said, "Sure," and pulled over, and I got out.

After they'd gone out of sight, I walked back to Joanne, and we talked.

Her life had gone totally downhill. She had more track marks on her arm than a CN Rail yard. Her teeth were bad, her hair was oily and greasy and scraggly, and her skin was pitted. I said, "What happened?" She said, "I got mixed up with the wrong people." She said she used to come and stand across from the Studio, wanting to come in and get help, but she'd been afraid that she might be rejected and she was afraid that her boyfriend would find out.

"You don't want to mess with my boyfriend. He's killed people." She said he wouldn't hesitate to hurt her somehow, or torch her place.

I said, "Joanne, you have to leave this city. Find somewhere else to live and don't tell a soul, including me, where you're going. Go to Toronto or someplace like that, and go straight to Social Services and get help. Maybe go to a recovery place or something like that, but start a new life. If you stay here, you'll probably never do that. It's not going to get better." She said, "You're probably right," and we parted company. I haven't seen her since. I don't feel much hope for what happened to her and I feel terrible guilt for sending her to the wolves in the first place. It makes me very sad to think of what happened to her.

There were a few sad things that happened for people at the Pacific Artists Studio, but for the most part it was great. It was a lot of fun and I look back on those days with a lot of pride because I was able to create that community, and I knew that 99 percent of the artists who went through there really liked me. I know this because many of them are still good friends of mine, and because of the number of times they've used me in their art.

For instance, there was this guy Graham Harrop, a cartoonist. He went on to become a cartoonist for the Globe and Mail, but at that time he was just another struggling artist. Graham took on the job of putting out the Pacific Artists Studio newsletter. He always drew cartoons that were included in the newsletter, and frequently he'd do a batch of cartoons that he'd put up on the walls around the studio. Several of them involved me with my dog.

To give you some background, I used to take my dog out for walks and I'd be wearing this fedora and a leather jacket I had with a fur collar. I wear a cowboy hat, now, but in those days it was a fedora. Anyway, if one of the artists was going out, sometimes I'd ask them if they'd take the dog with them for a walk. Graham did a cartoon that showed me asking one of the artists to take the dog out and pay their rent, too. In another one, he had the dog and me walking together, both of us wearing fedoras and fur collars.

Graham was an impish little man. He was older than I was, but he looked ten years younger and he acted like this little kid. He was a fantastic person and everybody loved him in that studio. So when he came to me one day and said he had to move out because he had no money, I told him he could stay for a month or two until he got back on his feet. He said, "Well I can't even pay the rent at home. I have to move out of my place, too." I told him he could stay in the hat check room for a while. The hat check room was a holdover from the old big band days. I had a few artists that spent time staying in the hat check room. One of them later became a teacher at Capilano College and now owns four houses in North Vancouver.

So Graham moved into the hat check room. Years later, when he got the job with the Globe and Mail, he made a copy of the first cartoon he did for them and sent it to me with a note that said I deserved it for helping him out. For 20 years he did a cartoon for the paper called "the Backbench," and recently put together a collection of those cartoons into a book that he has dedicated to me, saying he remembered how I helped him when things were down and out. So, that was a nice thing for him to do.

Another guy that used me in his art was the head pastry chef for the Four Seasons Hotel. He used to use the studio to do all his lard sculptures for the table centrepieces.

One day I came in and he was in the process of building a sculpture of a centaur—you know, half man and half horse. The figure had his arm up in the air and was looking at the sky. There were Roman pillars that had fallen around him and there was a nude woman lying across the bottom of the piece with a horse's leg over her.

I ignored it for a week or so, and then one day he said, "Gary, come here. I want to show you something. I've finally finished the sculpture. See what you think of it." I went over and looked at it and finally noticed it was me! He had put my head on it, with my face and hair and everything! Everybody came around to see and we all had a great laugh. He ended up giving it to me and it stayed in a showcase at the entrance to the studio for years. I kept waiting to see it melt, but it never did, although it did get a little yellowish in time. I think that just gave it a little more character. I always thought it would be cool to have a sculpture of oneself that was bronze or something. But no: my life? Lard.

Another guy who came into the Pacific Artists Studio was a fellow named Mike McKinnel who did many front covers for the Province and a lot of magazines. He had a field day with me. He did so many drawings that he said he could do me in his sleep. He did a clay sculpture of my head that was incredibly accurately detailed. It was a little freaky walking into the studio and looking at myself. Mike was a funny guy. He was the best man at my third marriage.

In many ways, the highlight for me—the event that more than anything else let me know how they felt about me—was the surprise party they threw for me when I turned 40 and the ring they made for me that I still wear today.

I was going out with a girl named Dusty at the time. Dusty was my dance partner as well as being my girlfriend, and that night she told me that she was going to take me out dancing and then for dinner for my birthday. We went dancing, and then before we went for dinner, she said we had to stop at the studio because she'd left something at my place that she needed.

We walked into the studio and it was dead quiet; there wasn't a soul around. Except for a few small lights at the back, it was dark. All of a sudden, the lights went on and I heard hundreds of people yelling, "Surprise!" Then they lifted up a banner that ran 100 feet along the wall that read: "Happy Birthday Gary." The signature went from one end to the other.

It was a huge party. There were two bands, and all the people from the gay club—patrons and all—came up. There were people everywhere; there had to be close to 800 people there that night. It was great.

At one point, we gathered in the lounge area and I opened up presents that they gave me. They held this one present till the very end and then they said, "This is from everybody in the Pacific Artists Studio." It was a ring they had designed, which was special enough, but they had made it out of several rings that I'd had in my jewellery box for a long time and that I'd said to someone that I should have melted and made into something good.

One of the artists was married to a jewellery maker, so she'd taken those rings and melted them down. The new ring was done as an artist's palette with inlaid stones. The thing about this ring, though, too, is that it not only represented that strong community, but it was also made from a ring that my dad had given to me and another that my second wife, Sylvia, had given me. It meant a lot and still does.

I made a lot of friends there, and a handful of us still get together today. I have nothing but wonderful memories of that place. It was a good studio, and probably one of the first and largest communal art communities under one roof in western Canada.

20 Heroes

The building housing the Pender Auditorium burned down in the summer of 2003. Not surprising, really. It was all wood slats and would never have met any modern fire codes. The fire itself was one of the biggest ever recorded in downtown Vancouver—you could see it from pretty much anywhere in the Greater Vancouver area. 339 Pender Street was a firetrap waiting to happen, but it was a heritage building and it's sad that it burned down. Fortunately, the mural had been moved long before.

The mural had been around since 1947, and over the years it had faded, and there was some water staining in the centre of it plus many cracks. It depressed me because first of all, I was born in 1947 and I hated to be reminded of my own aging in that way, but also we needed that wall to display the artists' work. We needed a big white wall. The building's owners told me they didn't care what I did with it, but with all of us in the studio being artists, we really respected the work and the labour history that it represented, so I kept putting off doing anything about it. Finally I figured I had to do something.

I learned that the artist who painted the mural, Fraser Wilson, was still alive, as was his assistant, Stan Billows, whose name was also on the mural. Fraser was 82 at the time; Stan had to be in his seventies. I called them, and they were happy to talk about the mural's very rich history.

Stan told me he had been a cartoonist working for a local newspaper in the mid-40s, a time of major union upheaval in the city of Vancouver. Stan had done a pro-union cartoon that ran in the paper, and as the paper was mainstream, it took a lot of flak from its advertisers and subscribers for carrying that cartoon. The paper asked Stan to do something supporting the anti-union position. He refused, and ended up being fired.

The Marine Workers and Boilermakers Union felt bad about that, so they made him a special member and commissioned him to do the mural in their building, depicting all the major union movements of the day like logging, fishing, mining, and ship-building. So in the mural there was a guy pushing logs on a log boom, there was a fishing boat, a car on tracks coming out of a mine shaft, a welder working on a ship, and factories in the distance on the North Shore. But like I said, it was in bad shape.

I wanted to save the mural somehow, so I contacted places like the City of Vancouver Archives, UBC, and the Vancouver Art Gallery and told them about it. Nobody was interested. They said I should just paint it over and not worry about it. But I couldn't, in clear conscience, paint the mural out because I thought, "There's got to be some kind of historical significance to it. It's part of Vancouver's history."

As a last effort, I called up a reporter working for CBC-TV, told her about the situation and asked her to let the public know that if someone didn't do something about the mural within a month, it would be painted over and a valuable part of the city's history would be gone. She was concerned, and promised to get the story on the air.

The very next day the mayor at the time, Mike Harcourt—along with city councillors Harry Rankin and Bruce Eriksen and a bunch of union people—came knocking on my door. They came in, saw the mural, and of course were insistent that I not paint it out. They said they'd try to do something, and asked me how much I wanted for the mural. I said I'd sell it to them for one dollar if they would put a brand new plasterboard wall up for me and paint it white, and compensate the artists in the studio for the length of time it took to put up that wall. They agreed. I gave them the name of some people who were professional mural restorers and had been tenants at one time. They agreed.

The restorers arrived, along with some labourers as well as the two painters, Fraser Wilson and Stan Billows, and the process of taking the mural out began.

First they cut out the four-by-eight–foot plasterboard panels that formed the larger piece. They took them down very gently and wrapped each thoroughly with bubble wrap. Then they carried them downstairs and put them on a flatbed truck out front. They took it to the Maritime Labour Centre, where it was restored and where it now stands. During the restoration process, part of the painting became damaged, and they actually got Fraser Wilson to repaint that part.

And we got our white wall. Everyone was happy.

The next thing that happened was I received an invitation to come to the Maritime Labour Centre at Triumph and Victoria because they were going to unveil the new mural. All of the politicians were there, as well as the two painters. They pulled the strings and the curtains opened and there was this big bronze plaque beside the mural and there right at the top of the plaque, where the donors were credited, was the Pacific Artists Studio and my name. I had no idea they were going to do that.

That was in 1988. The following year I moved out of the building and met my third wife, Tracy.

Well, I didn't exactly just move out: I was evicted. The city by-law guys came and said they'd received a report that I'd been living on the premises. They said the building was allowed only one resident suite, and that was for the caretaker. I figured it was actually the caretaker who reported me, because he'd taken a strong dislike to me ever since the tenants began coming to me with their problems rather than him. I think he also had a problem with artists. And, of course, I wasn't supposed to be living there. I wasn't, however, the only person to live there illegally. In fact, when the building burned down long after I'd gone, there was believed to be four artists still living there.

Anyway, they gave me 48 hours to find a place, so I had to do some quick looking. Fortunately, money wasn't too much of an issue right then, and I found a pretty decent place in a quiet neighbourhood. I had the penthouse—a suite built on top of a three-story walk-up.

From up there I had a good view of what went on below, and there was a really pretty woman I used to see walking out of the building. One day when I saw her walking out to the sidewalk, I flew down the back stairs, ran down the lane and was able to meet her as she came around the corner of the block.

I said, "Oh, hi. Don't you live in that building up on 12th there?"

"Yes, I do."

"Well, I live in the penthouse in that building."

"Oh, right," she said. "I think I've seen you around a couple of times."

She told me she was on her way to catch the bus, and as my car had broken down and I had to go to work, I could say truthfully that I was doing the same, and so we walked to the bus stop together.

I told her what I did and invited her to come down, kind of laying it on, you know, saying I could give her a tour of the artists' studios and that kind of stuff. She agreed, and within three days we were dating. We really hit it off. Within a week, she was spending a lot of time at my place, and finally I said, "You might as well move up here because that's an awfully expensive closet you have down there." Not too long after, we got married. The marriage didn't last, but to this day we are the greatest friends. We probably should have stayed good friends rather than getting married.

Anyway, the next event happened during that period. It was definitely a day to remember.

I had picked up Tracy from her work and we'd headed home. When we got there, we noticed that our front door had been smashed in and we'd been robbed—all of our jewellery and money was gone. The police came and did a report, and then the landlord showed up and promised to fix the door. (This is not the big story).

I said to Tracy, "Look, they're going to be banging while they fix the door and everything. There's no point in cooking. Let's go out for dinner." She thought this was a good idea and we headed out again. (Now the main story begins).

We had driven a couple of blocks when I saw a group of people standing on the curb, and they were all looking at a building across the street. I looked over and I could see smoke coming out of a spot on the rim of the building. I thought, "That's a weird place for a chimney," so I pulled over. By then I was able to see flames flickering over the edge of the building. I asked the people watching whether anybody had let the people in the building know that their building was on fire. They didn't know.

So I ran across the street and hit the buzzer. A woman answered and I said, "Let me into the building and get yourself out because the building is on fire." She went, "Yeah, right."

She didn't believe me. I said, "Ma'am, if you don't do it, I'm going to break the glass and come in the front door and pull the alarm." She said, "Are you serious?" I said, "I am dead serious." So she let me in.

I started running around the building knocking on doors, seeing who was home and telling those that were to get out. By the time I reached the second floor, this other guy came running up. He said he was a cab driver and offered to help. I told him that I hadn't notified anyone in the basement, so he went down there and I continued knocking on doors on the second and third floors. Fortunately, there were only the three floors.

The third floor was filled with smoke, and I could see that most of it was coming from a door at the end of the hall. I knocked on a few of the other doors on that side, but nobody answered, so I figured nobody was at home. By this time, the smoke was billowing through the door of the place on fire. I had roughly three feet of clearance on the floor where there was no smoke, but I was coughing and sputtering. I finally got to the last door and knocked and this little old lady answered the door. She went, "Oh my goodness. Oh my goodness." I said, "Come on. We've got to get out of here." She said, "I haven't got my walker. I can't walk down the stairs." I said, "Never mind. I'll carry you down."

So I grabbed her around the waist and picked her up. She was quite a frail lady so she was very light. I said, "Just bury your head in my neck here," and put my elbow against the wall to guide me, and then just followed the wall until I could see the glowing exit light through the smoke. I was fumbling around and coughing, but I finally got the door open and we got down the stairwell and out the back door. People out there were applauding when we walked out. I made sure she was okay, and then I went and sat on the curb. By then the firemen had arrived and they gave me oxygen (and a good dose of praise and stuff).

A newspaper reporter was there and he asked if he could do an interview with me the next day. We arranged to meet at the Studio, but he called the next day to say that the smoke had been cleared from the building, and we ended up doing the interview there along with the woman that I'd rescued.

The next morning there we are in the Vancouver Sun, this lady and me. We're sitting on her couch and the caption is saying something about how I'll always be her hero.

Later I was even given an award for doing that bit of rescue work.

▲ A model and Maynard, the cat that gave me the idea for Cinemazoo

▲ Me with a unicorn during the filming of *Teen Mom, Teen Rebel*

▲ With a bald eagle, Surrey, BC, 2004

▲ A day spent wrangling frogs for a Mitsubishi commercial, from footage shot for the *Saving Cinemazoo* web series

▲ My very favourite snake that I was forced to ship out of the province

▲ My huskies: Cinemazoo's highest-earning dogs. Whistler, BC, 2008

▲ A chimp moment: Bernie and Louie
photo taken by Thomas Kitchin

▲ Up at Whistler with two of my falcons

▲ Me and Brettony
photo taken by Tamiko Spicer

▲ Pastel commission of German Shepherd; my own work

▲ With a sheep in New York City—a great way to meet people!

▲ Gary the Buffalo Hunter,
pastel by Margaret Milligan

▲ A caricature of me done during
the Boat for Hope event, by Mark
Stiemaczeski, 2011

▲ My own royal souvenir,
watercolour by John Neilly, 1982

▲'50 Ways to Leave Your Hat On,'
mixed media, by Mike McKinnell

▲ Oil painting by Mike McKinnell, 2007

▲ Me and Jag

(This story is not over yet).

The next thing that happens is that I get a call from one of the local radio talk-show hosts, Rafe Mair, asking if I'd come to the station for an interview. So I go in, and he does about a ten-minute interview with me. He wants to know what made me do what I did and whether I had worried about my own safety. I tell him it all happened so fast I didn't even think about what I was doing. His parting question is: "What does it feel like to be a hero?" I say, "You know what? I don't have any feelings about it, because I don't think it was heroism. I think heroism is when you can actually see that your life is at risk and you still do what you do. And anyway, I didn't go through flames. I went through smoke, but I didn't feel it was a huge risk." (Story's not over).

A few months later, I get an invitation to attend a presentation at the UBC Women's Club. Tracy and I go, and I'm expecting maybe it has to do with saving the lady's life. We get there and it's all pretty formal. They escort us to a table, and then awhile later they escort someone else to our table. I look up and it's Bryan Adams. He's here for some kind of music award. I'm thinking, "Cool." We sit and talk for awhile, and then they get to the awards being presented by then-mayor Gordon Campbell. You can imagine my surprise when he announces that "The next award is for the preservation of historical art for the City of Vancouver, and it goes to Gary Oliver." It's for the mural!

(The story's still not over).

Some time later, I was doing some work in Saskatchewan and I was at the airport there. It was very early in the morning and I was sitting in the waiting area with my arms crossed, kind of dozing off, when all of a sudden I felt a whack in the back of my neck.

I turned around and here it was Harry Rankin, one of the councillors involved with saving the mural. He said, "How are you doing, Gary?" I said, "Just fine." So he sat down and we started talking. He said, "You know, that was quite the thing you did." I said, "What?" He went, "The mural, of course." Harry was a real union guy. He said, "And you got that award too, for saving the lady. That means you're going to be in the City Archives. You know some people go their whole lives without making it into the City Archives, and you're already in there twice."

So that's the story of how I saved a mural and a lady and became a hero. Strange the way life works.

21 A Camera and a Cat

Those kinds of things made me feel good, but otherwise I was starting to get that feeling again that time was slipping by and I wasn't really going anywhere. It was 1991; I'd been running the Pacific Artists Studio for over a decade, and while it was a great place and I was proud of what I'd accomplished there, I still felt something was missing. Besides, I needed money. Once all the expenses were paid—like rent for the space, hydro and telephone bills and a receptionist, plus my own living expenses—there wasn't a lot left over. I was pulling in a bit extra from the photography, but not enough, and doing photography was feeling stagnant. So when my mom introduced me to a fellow who owned an art supply company in Quebec and needed a salesperson, I was open to hearing more.

My mom had given him a good description of my background selling art supplies, both with my dad and on my own, and he was impressed. He offered me a financial arrangement: salary plus commissions that I couldn't refuse, and to top it off, he'd supply a vehicle. I would still run the Pacific Artists Studio, but I'd make good money on the side selling art supplies to companies in western Canada.

With the connections I already had as well as new ones I made, by the end of a year I had worked my way up to being one of the highest-earning salespersons in the company. But

I wasn't enjoying it. I was travelling a lot—like, three weeks out of every month on the road. It meant being away from Tracy, and I also wasn't able to do a good job of managing the Pacific Artists Studio. It was hard to collect rent from the artists when I wasn't around. I mean, they were artists—if they could get away without paying rent, they would. Beyond that, though, I knew the job just wasn't my cup of tea.

I struggled through for another half year. The money was getting even better, but I was enjoying it less and less. Finally, I rationalized that if I stayed with the company, I was going to become more and more dependent on that money. I'd probably buy a house, maybe get a cottage, get a fancy car. I mean, the money was *that* good. I didn't want to get to a place where I couldn't leave the company because I needed the money to support the lifestyle I'd created. So I handed in my letter of resignation.

My poor mom almost had a cardiac arrest. She said, "You need psychological help, you know?" She was devastated by what I'd done.

"Do you have another job to go to?

"No."

"Well, why would you leave a good job like this?"

"Because I'm not happy doing it."

"Well, what are you going to do?

"I've still got the art studio, and I can pick up the photography again."

"But Gary, you just barely made ends meet with that. It's not a secure job. You've got no benefits, nothing."

I said, "You know what? I don't know what it is, but there's something out there that has my name on it, and I'll find it. I will find it someday and, when I do, I'll know. It will be a job that'll make me happy and I'll love doing it, whether I make money or not. I want to be happy."

She heard me, but said, "I wish you would reconsider."

The company brought me out to the head office to talk about it. They offered me more money and a better car, and offered to make me head of sales for the company. I was incredibly tempted to stay. I said, "I'm going back to Vancouver. I'll think about it and give you an answer in two days."

I was already thinking I didn't want it by the time I got home, but I thought perhaps I wasn't being sensible, so I debated it with myself for a couple of days and then finally said, "No."

My mom was even more devastated. She said, "I can't believe it. I just can't believe it."

I went back to running the Studio, and I called up some of the models I'd done work for before and told them I was back in business doing fashion photography.

One day not long after, Judy—one of the models I'd worked with many times—came into the studio. She told me she needed some new shots, and she wanted a shot of her with Maynard (the studio's cat) for her portfolio. This was not an unusual request; most of the models wanted Maynard in at least one of their shots.

Maynard was a very special cat. I'd named him after the character on television, Maynard G. Krebs on the show "The Many Loves of Doby Gillis." Maynard G. Krebs was the most laid-back, easygoing, mellow type of guy. He couldn't say the word "work" because it wasn't in his vocabulary.

Maynard was that kind of a cat, just really loveable and laid-back. He got along with everybody, loved people. During open houses, when we might get up to 800 guests, Maynard would be right in there socializing with everyone. All the artists kept a spot in their space for Maynard to sleep. To this day I still get asked about that cat.

Anyway, Maynard loved the camera. If he knew I had the camera out, especially if he saw a flash go off, he'd run to get in front of the camera lickety-split. One time I even had a stuffed wild boar in the shoot and he jumped on the back of it to pose. Another time there was a lightning storm, and Maynard was running all over the studio looking for the camera so he could pose.

So Judy wants to pose with Maynard. We set up the scene and she's posing with him and Maynard is licking her face and Judy says: "You know what? You should get this cat working in the film industry or in advertising or something." I said, "Yeah, that's a good idea." There were three spaces empty in the studio at the time and the added income would be very welcome.

Vancouver has a healthy film industry. It's more active now, but even then Vancouver was a sought-after location for shooting feature films. We're known as "Hollywood North." So I started phoning people in the film industry and asking if they knew of an animal agent. They all said, "No. We only know animal wranglers." So I asked them to give me the name of a wrangler. I called him up and said, "I have a cat that just loves being photographed. It'll pose for hours in front of a camera."

He said, "Oh? What kind of cat?"

"It's a tabby—a silver tabby with big blue eyes."

Then he asked for my name and phone number and said, "Well, if we need a tabby cat, we'll give you a call."

I said, "Don't you want to see the cat?"

"No," he said, "We know what a tabby cat looks like."

"Well, do you want some photos to show to your clients?"

"Nope, we can describe him."

"How can you describe him? You haven't even seen him!"

"It's a tabby cat, isn't it?

I called other wranglers in town and got this same response.

Their attitude bugged me, so I started looking in other cities. I'd go to the library and look in different city archives for wranglers or animal agents. I found extensive catalogues listing services for the film industry. I could find agents in those listings, and under agents I could find wranglers, but no agents for animals.

That's when the light went on. Maybe I should open up an agency for animals!

By then I knew a lot about how modelling agencies worked. I knew what was involved in recruiting models and in producing a strong portfolio. I knew how to produce the kind of photographs that promoted models. Why not do the same for animals?

I didn't know yet that this was to be the job, but I was very excited by the idea.

Then one day, one of the artists said, "Hey, Gary. I hear you're opening up some kind of animal talent agency." I go, "Yeah, I'm thinking about it."

"Really!"

"Yeah."

"What are you going to call it?"

"I'm thinking maybe Noah's Animal Agents."

"Are you going to have animals of your own?"

"Knowing me, I'll probably have a zoo."

"So you're going to have your own zoo for the cinema."

"Yeah, my own cinema zoo."

As soon as I said it I thought, "That's the name. That's it. Cinemazoo."

22 It's a Zoo!

So I had the idea. Now what?

I figured the first thing I needed to do was to find a place to put the animals when I got them. I couldn't run a zoo out of the Pacific Artists Studio, plus it was never long before the empty spaces had been rented and I had a waiting list. I noticed an empty building that was just a couple of blocks down from the studio, so I found out who the realtors were and learned that they were managing the property. I went to talk with them, but sensing that they might not be that excited about having a bunch of animals in their building, I told them that I was looking to rent the space to handle the overflow of artists from the Pacific Artists Studio, that I had decided to move over the artists who were more involved in commercial art. That part was, in fact, true, but I thought it would impress them, too. I also said that I wanted to get another business going, not mentioning exactly what business. I added that I had a pretty solid track record with this kind of thing, that I'd been running the Pacific Artists Studio for 12 years and had a waiting list and all. I was pretty convincing. And then I added the gambit that had worked so well at the Pender Auditorium building: "If you're willing to give me a couple of months rent free, maybe I can get something going here too."

Given that the building had been empty for a couple of years, it wasn't surprising that the guy said, "Sure, no problem."

I put an ad in the paper that said that Cinemazoo, Canada's first animal agency, was opening its doors at 539 Hamilton Street the following Saturday at 9:00 am, and that anyone who wanted to see their animal in film and television should bring them to the agency at that time. That next Saturday morning, I was driving Tracy to her job at the Four Seasons Hotel and I decided to stop at the office and pick something up on the way, so I was driving down Hamilton Street. We noticed this long line of people. First of all, I wondered what the line-up was for. Then I said, "Hey, everybody has animals! They're coming to my place!" Sure enough, the line-up stretched from Dunsmuir—an avenue about a block from my office—all the way to my office door. There must have been around 200 people!

"Oh my God," I thought. How am I going to do portfolios on all of these people?" I had one roll of film. I was only expecting maybe two or three people! I said to Tracy, "What am I going to do? I don't have enough film."

So what I did was I dropped Tracy off at work and then I raced to a photo-finishing place on Hastings owned by a friend of mine. I said, "Robert, quick, give me a case of film and I promise I'll bring the money back later!" So he gave me a case and I went back and met the mob.

I worked until almost one o'clock in the morning. Really. People stayed that long to get their animals signed up. I was working by myself, so there I was trying to photograph the animals and make sure all the recruitment forms were filled in and trying to devise a system on the spot to keep track of whose photos were which on which roll. I'd never had more than three at a time doing fashion photography, so that had never really been a problem before. I was going mental trying to figure out how to do it all. What an introduction!

And it just kept coming for days after. I was thinking, "Man, have I hit a gold mine." Then it began petering out and I had a chance to take stock. One of the first things I did was hire an assistant: Danine. Danine was actually president of the Association of Reptile Keepers; I'd met her one time at the Pacific National Exhibition. When I told her about Cinemazoo, she said, "Boy, I'd love to work for your company," and so I hired her.

The next priority was to get a portfolio together of all those animals that would include pertinent information about them as well as their photos. And then, the big test—to take that portfolio around to the various production companies and advertising agencies and find work for the animals.

I learned pretty quickly that it was not going to be as easy as I thought.

23 Becoming Jim

Since I started Cinemazoo, I've had all kinds of adventures that I never dreamed would happen. Most involved animals, but some just had to do with being in business and surviving. Of course, that didn't start with Cinemazoo—I learned a lot about surviving with the Pacific Artists Studio as well. I got pretty good at convincing artists they should stay. I made sure it was a good place for them to be, but I also made sure I continued to get rent.

The same with Cinemazoo. There've been many times I've had to adapt in order to survive.

For instance, I never intended to be a wrangler. Yes, I had fantasized about being Jim on "Wild Kingdom" when I was a kid, but in reality, I didn't think I was qualified to wrangle animals. I did feel qualified to be their agent, and that was what I was going to be. My business plan was that I would be their agent and I would form alliances with professional wranglers to do the actual work with the animals on-set.

Shortly after I opened Cinemazoo, I read in the newspaper about a woman who was a wrangler, so I called her up. I said, "Hey, you know I'm opening up an animal agency. I'm wondering whether you would be interested in an arrangement where I line up the jobs and the animals, and you charge me your normal fee for wrangling, and I put a percentage on top for the client."

Well, that person tore a strip off me. She yelled and screamed at me, and told me that I was taking away her bread and butter. She said I had no right, coming into BC with this kind of fly-by-night idea. Who was I to do this? What experience did I have? She threatened to put me out of business in three months. She said, "You won't have a chance to exist in this business."

I was stunned, but I said, "Hey, I'm not trying to take your work away from you. I'm trying to enhance what you're doing." But she would hear nothing of it and hung up on me.

Well, of course my heart sank. I thought, "What the heck am I getting myself into here? What chance do I have if this is the kind of reaction I'm going to get?" I couldn't believe the level of paranoia. It was really discouraging and gave me thoughts like "What's the point?" for maybe a day.

Then I decided that I had a right to do this, too. Nobody can tell me how I feel about animals and about being in this industry. It made me really angry that someone would be that way. In my mind, I told that woman: "Someday you'll be sorry you took this attitude, because not only am I going to stay in business, I'm going to become a wrangler and learn what it takes to do this."

But that woman—and the other three or four wranglers in town—succeeded in making it difficult for me to get into the business, because the big film sets were staffed by union members and they were the only voting members in the union that controlled animal wrangling in the film industry. No matter what I did to gain union status, they voted me out. The union wasn't that happy about the situation, but there wasn't much they could do. I'm pretty sure the other wranglers were influenced by the person I spoke with on the phone that day, but it made it a pretty closed shop.

The other thing they did was refuse to use any of my animals in their work. It was really silly, too, because I specialized in the small animals while they were handling the big animals like lions and tigers and bears. One time I actually complained to the union about the situation, and they said they'd put out a memo to the wranglers saying that if they didn't have the animals in question, to check with me first. They said, "Then you can at least supply them with the animals even if you can't wrangle on set." I went, "Cool. That's great." But they never did call.

And it went to ridiculous lengths, like the time one of them had to supply a chameleon for an advertising shoot. I had at least half a dozen really nice, healthy, good-looking chameleons.

I know the wrangler had been told to come to me, but she went to Victoria—can you imagine? all the way to Victoria—to get herself a chameleon. The sad icing on this particular cake was that the chameleon died on set and the wrangler tried to blame it on the chameleon. She said the chameleon had ticks. I just laughed, because that's like saying your dog died because it had fleas. It just didn't make sense. Personally, I think that wrangler didn't have any experience working with reptiles and overworked the animal, stressed it. Chameleons are very, very sensitive.

Not being able to become a union member was a major barrier to my ability to get work in much of the feature film industry, but I thought, "Well, there are lots of independent films and other non-union jobs. I'll diversify." And that's how I survived: by diversifying, and of course, by being able to see and be open to new opportunities and act on them.

I started getting work, and 20 years later I'm still in business and I'm still wrangling. So there.

* * *

The first job I ever got working in feature films was for a movie called "Bird on a Wire," starring Goldie Hawn and Mel Gibson. It turned out it was a union film, but I didn't know that at the time. I soon found out.

I learned about the job when one of the directors called me up and asked if I could supply animals for the film. I, of course, said, "Sure. No problem." He said they needed a whole long list of animals including reptiles and big cats and primates and even vultures. Could I get them? I said, "Okay, fine. I can get them."

I brought in what animals I had myself, and otherwise went to all my resources and source books and asked owners to come in with their specialties. I found a fellow in Alberta who brought in the big cats—a tiger, a lion, and a jaguar. There was another guy in Santa Fe. I brought the big snakes, like my large Burmese python (needed for a scene with Goldie Hawn), and I had many of the birds like the budgies and doves and a pigeon. I found a large monitor lizard and I supplied a fairly large iguana we called Stanley.

When I first came on set, I was really excited. My first job working in the features! But people were treating me really badly. I was getting the cold shoulder and all these dirty looks. I couldn't believe how they were treating me. I thought, "What the heck did I do? What's wrong here?" Then finally, somebody told me that there was another wrangler—the same one who said she'd put me out of business—who'd just been kicked off the set because she'd gotten into a major conflict with one of the key people in the movie. I had been hired to replace her, and—it being a union set—me and the other guys I'd brought in were considered scabs.

It went from bad to worse. Next thing I knew, I was being threatened. Finally, one of the directors went to the union and said, "Look, this is our choice. We have no alternative. We can't work with the wrangler that you supplied, so we either do it with this wrangler or I guess we move our set." I heard they were prepared to move down to Seattle and rebuild their set there. Keep in mind we're talking about a multimillion-dollar set. The union swallowed any objections they might have had and we got on with making the movie.

It got better. What helped out a lot were Mel and Goldie, both of them. Goldie started bringing her daughter Caitlin down to the compound where I had the animals. I think Caitlin—she's called Kate now—was only about ten at the time. Goldie would ask if I minded if Caitlin hung around because she loved animals, could I keep an eye on her? I didn't mind, so Caitlin would hang around all day and play with the animals and then hook up later with Goldie.

And then I became friendly with Mel. This happened one day when I was in the food line with my assistant Danine, and Mel was just ahead of Danine in the line. Danine got a baked potato and she said, "Oh no, I wanted a mashed potato!" I said, "Oh, I'll take the baked potato," but as I reached for it Mel took my hand and squished it down into her baked potato. He said, "There. Now it's mashed." So I flicked the potato on my hand at him, and from then the war was on. He and I started doing water fights and balloon fights and all kinds of things. We got into trouble one time because I'd kind of soaked him just when his make-up was freshly done. That didn't go over well with the director, but all in all we had a lot of fun.

The thing is, once the key actors warmed up to me, everybody just sort of relaxed and accepted the fact that I was there. We were on set for 17 days and it all went well.

I learned a lot doing that movie, and what I learned served me well in the years ahead. I haven't worked on too many feature sets because of the union issue, but I've still worked on several since then.

Number one—and anyone who's worked in films can attest to this—is you have to learn to stay away from the food trucks. No, really, I gained so much weight on that first set because I'm an eater and they had all this food there. You could keep eating all day, and I think I did; especially those days when there was a lot of sitting around, because there's a lot of that, just sitting and waiting until your scene. So when I wasn't taking care of the animals—making sure they were stimulated and exercised and fed properly—I think I was eating.

I also learned about set protocol. This is important. You need to learn pretty quickly who the main players are on the set. Who you go to for different things and who calls the shots—literally in this case. Truly it's that kind of stuff that is the hardest part of wrangling.

As far as working with the animals, if you understand their nature—and this applies especially to exotic animals like the ones I work with most, the reptiles and spiders and turtles and such— then it's a matter of manipulating the animal to do what you want it to do. It's not about training, it's about manipulation.

Like people say, "How do you train a tarantula spider to do things like walk in a certain direction?" Well, if you know that tarantulas don't like any kind of wind or breeze, then you know you can use that kind of force to move the tarantula. The thing is that a lot of people think that tarantulas use their fangs to protect themselves, but this isn't the case. Their fangs are used to inject venom into their prey to break down solid to liquid matter so they can eat it easier. Their protection is actually their hair. Using their hind legs, they'll flick their abdomens, dislodging the hair, that then floats in the air and gets in the predator's eyes and starts to sting. While the predator is trying to get the hairs out of its eyes, the tarantula escapes. So the hair on their body is so loosely lodged that a good stiff wind will dislodge it.

If we have a tarantula on set and we want it to move in a certain direction, all I do is get a canister of compressed air and blow it toward the spider to get it to move away. If I do it slowly, he'll move away slowly. If I give it a good blast, away he goes.

Same kind of thing applies to a snake. Enemies attack snakes from behind because they don't want to get too close to the mouth. As soon as the snake realizes there's something behind it, it'll move away so it can get in a better position for control. So if I touch the snake's tail, he'll move forward. You can't always predict the direction and it might take a take or two, but you'll get it to move where you want to go eventually.

When it comes to the more dangerous animals like alligators and rattlesnakes, there's a set protocol that I learned first by reading books and then by experience over the years, and I learn from others who know. I only handle animals I'm familiar with, so if I have to supply an unfamiliar animal, I bring in experts to work with them and then I learn from them. Like, when I was doing "Bird on a Wire," the wranglers for the big cats were the guys who brought them in. But I helped, and I learned.

These days I have my own collection of very dangerous animals, but I know how to work with them. I use all the safety precautions. I do not want to go out like Steve Irwin. I think Steve was an amazing enthusiast about animals—he loved them with a passion that was unbelievable—but he took his chances. I think everyone who knew him expected that he was probably going to go out working with animals. Me? I'm not going to jump into a swamp when I know there's an alligator in there but I can't see it, nor am I going to pick up a deadly poisonous snake and hold it close to my face saying, "Isn't this beautiful," you know? I want to know exactly where the animal is and have the proper equipment to deal with it. If it's a venomous snake, I want a hook, and I don't plan on picking up anything like that unless it's absolutely necessary. I know I said I wanted to be Jim, but frankly, I've learned that being right in there with the animals can hurt.

I've had friends who have been killed by animals. One was a friend who was keeping some venomous snakes for me. The man was an expert. He was retired at the time the incident happened, but he'd been working with snakes all his life and had over 300 snakes of his own. For some reason, he reached into a tank holding one of my cobras—why he put his hand in that tank and how he got tagged by the cobra is still unclear—and it killed him. The situation was made worse, because he had asthma and must have panicked because he knew the effect of the venom would be worse for him. I heard he couldn't even make it out to the sidewalk to get help. I know that if you make a mistake like that, putting your bare hand into a tank with a venomous snake, it can be your last.

I've had some pretty close encounters myself that I would not want to repeat. Perhaps the worst was one time when a woman came to Cinemazoo wanting to see the animals. I gave her a tour, but kept the snakes to the last because she was quite scared of snakes. At the time I kept two Burmese pythons in a room that was an old vault, about ten feet long and seven feet wide, that you entered from a larger room. The snake vault was escape-proof, so they were free to roam, and I'd created an environment that gave them branches to climb on and such. The pythons were large—the female was 18 feet long, the male was 16 feet—but they were really tame. I handled them almost daily.

We get to the snake room and I'm squatting down in the doorway with the woman behind me. I have my hands cupped together resting in my lap and I'm talking over my shoulder to her, telling her about these snakes. The female, Christine, is approaching me slowly, but I really don't think anything of it. I turn around to say something to the woman and Christine strikes. She gets both my hands in her mouth and within seconds has coiled around my arms and popped my left shoulder out of its socket. So, there I am with this snake coiled on me. I can't use my hands to get her off because my hands are going down her throat.

The woman said, "What are you doing?" I said, "Well, I'm in a bit of a situation here." I knew it was serious. I knew this snake had many feet left on her and I couldn't let her use the rest of her body to coil around my waist or my neck or I'd be history.

So I told the woman, "The snake has a hold of me and it's serious, so can you go out and get help?" She cried, "Oh my God! Oh my God!" I said, "Don't panic. I need you now." So she said, "Okay, okay," and ran out.

When she did, she closed the door to the outer room and it locked behind her. I couldn't turn the handle to get out, and she couldn't get back in.

So there I am, stuck with this snake. I'm not panicking, but my body breaks out in a sweat. I know I'm in very serious trouble. And I'm bleeding like anything—there's blood pouring out of my arms, because of course she's squeezing my arms really tight, which forces the blood up into my hand where she's biting me. I have a white shirt on to boot, so I know I look pretty bad. All I can do is try to keep the snake occupied by moving around so her attention stays focused on trying to grip other things with her tail instead of around me.

I heard a knocking on the outer door. "Gary, there's nobody in the building and your door is locked." I said, "Okay, go and find somebody outside. Phone 911 and tell them what's happening.

Don't hesitate to break the door down." She went off again.

I'm thinking, "I have to do something. What can I do?" I'm looking around the main room, which is about 20 feet long, and my eyes focus on the room at the end where we have a bear claw bathtub we use for grooming the dogs. I know the water can get scalding hot real fast. I figure if I can get the snake down and into the bathtub and then kick on the hot water, she might let go of me. So I drag her over to the bathtub—and believe me, it's a battle because she's constantly trying to hook onto something and squeezing tighter as she does—but I get her down to the room.

What I don't remember is how I was able to lift her up and get her into the bathtub, because she weighed 225 pounds. I think it was pure adrenaline that me made able to do it, considering my shoulder was out of its socket and I had lost a lot of blood by then. But she was in the tub, which fortunately had those old-fashioned faucets with cross handles, and I managed to kick on the hot water with my foot. Once it got hot, I sort of slid her down into it and then she began fighting to get out. She freaked, absolutely freaked. She uncoiled from me and just wanted out. She knew having my hands in her mouth was hurting her, so she uncoiled and literally threw me out of her mouth. I fell against the wall and just felt everything rip.

I scrambled out of the bathing room and ran out of the door of the main room into the hallway. Nobody was there yet. Down the hall I had another little room where I kept cleaning supplies, so I grabbed a towel and wrapped it around the arm that seemed the worst. There was blood all over my arms, my shirt, my face and on the ground.

I stood there and tried to compose myself, then slowly unwrapped the towel to see if she had hit an artery. She hadn't.

Then I heard crashing back in that room. Christine was trying to get out herself, so I knew I had to try to get her back in the vault. I went in and threw a towel over her head then reached down and grabbed her around the neck. It was awkward because I could only do it with one hand because of my shoulder, which was now giving me a lot of pain.

As I grabbed her by the neck, I got dizzy because I was all bent over, and I felt like I was going to pass out so I kind of slid down the doorjamb and was sitting holding her on my lap with the towel over her head. That calmed her down, too. The two of us were sitting there when my next-door neighbour in the office came in. He owned a company that supplied ambulances with medical supplies. Too bad he wasn't one of the ambulance guys. Anyway, he walked in and saw me sitting there, covered in blood, and he said, "Are you okay?" I said, "Yeah, I think so." He couldn't really see the snake at first, but as he looked closer he could see the body of the snake coming out behind me. He went, "Oh my God, that thing is huge!" I took the towel off and told him not to worry, that I had a firm grip on its head. He said, "Oh, Gary, I am really—" (he used a four-letter word here,) "—afraid of snakes." I told him: "Well, I really need you to get yourself together here, because we've got to get this snake back in its cage."

"Where is that?"

"The other end of the room."

"What do you want me to do?"

"Crawl over top of me and grab her tail. We don't have to pick her up, we just have to drag her, but I need you to keep her tail free from any objects she could hold onto as we go through the studio."

So we started to glide her back to the vault. I got her halfway through the door of the vault and as soon as she sensed she was in her own area, she stopped struggling and we were able to put her down—tail first—and then I put her head down. I patted her on her side and she slithered into her room. I closed the door and just thought, "Oh . . . my . . . God."

My neighbour took a look at my wounds and offered to go get some supplies to clean them up. I was soaking wet with blood and sweat, so I said I'd go outside and sit on the retainer wall outside the building to get some fresh air. "You do that," he said.

So he went off and got some Savlon and then came back, and was pouring it over my hands when the ambulance showed up. Of course they knew each other.

The ambulance guy yells out from the truck: "Are you the one that was bit by the snake?" I go, "Yeah." He looks at the other guy and says, "He looks like he's been hit by a truck." He says, "Where are you hurt?" I say, "Well, my shoulder, for one, and the bites on my arms."

"How big was that snake?"

"18 feet."

He says, "No disrespect or anything, but where is the snake now?"

When I told him the snake was locked up in its room, he said, "Okay, we can get out now."

They knocked my shoulder back into place, which hurt a lot, and then they bandaged me up. I needed some stitches, but I just went to a clinic to get that done. However, just as the ambulance guys were leaving, up drove a SWAT team.

They get out with guns and masks on, yelling, "Where's the snake?" I say, "Whoa, guys, relax. It's put away, locked up. And it doesn't have an Uzi." It was a pretty silly scene.

Then one cop asked to see the snake, so I took him upstairs and opened the door. He looked in and went, "Wow, they are amazing." And he went on and on talking about them and asking questions until I said, "You know what? If you want to come back tomorrow, I'll give you a tour. Right now, I think I'd better get to the doctor and get these things stitched." He said, "Oh, I'm sorry! Yeah, you go ahead." People are always fascinated by these animals.

But the big lesson for me was "always wash your hands before you go in to be with another animal." See, I'd forgotten that I'd been handling a guinea pig earlier when I'd been taking the woman around on the tour, and it had had a bit of a wet bottom. I had dried my hand, probably on my jeans, but I still had this strong scent of urine from the guinea pig on my hand when we reached the snakes. I should have known better—it was a stupid thing for me to do, because Christine just did what was natural for her.

Most snakes are creatures of habit. I'd had Christine for 11 years and for all that time, she'd seen me come into her room with food in my hand, usually something dead like a mouse or rat. I'd throw it on the floor and she'd take it and eat it. In this case, I'd opened the door to her room, so she was anticipating she was going to get fed, and then she'd smelled the guinea pig on my hand and thought it was food for her. It's why people should not reach into a snake cage with their hands. Snakes are anticipating food, and they can't see well so their aim can be bad. If you're holding food out with your hand, like a mouse or something, your hand can become the victim.

It was certainly a lesson I never forgot again but the experience was important in another way too. I learned that in a situation like that, I was able to stay calm and composed and basically do the right things.

Basically, you know, when you're working with animals, you're going to be okay as long as you use common sense. Stop and think about what you're doing. Think, "What would be the animal's reaction to what I'm doing?" If you don't know that animal's nature; if you don't understand its habits, you shouldn't be working with it. If you're just guessing—or alternately, over-confident—you can get tagged. The best way is to know the animal, use common sense, have patience, and be clearly in charge.

Now, on set, if the animal's owner is there, that can pose problems. For example, if the pet is a dog and is halfway through the scene and sees its owner, it may begin to head over to him or her. In those cases, I'll usually ask the owner to go to the green room, and then I'll get their input on what works best with their pet and go back out and take over. Usually that works fine. If, however, I think the owner can handle the animal better because they're more familiar with it, then I'm happy to let the owner get the animal back in line. Wranglers are always saying they don't want the owners around, but I think if the animal responds better to the owner, well, then, why not let them be involved? We're all there to get the job done.

One thing, though: if you're working on set, don't let yourself be pressured to make the animals do things that are not good for it. You know what your animal's capabilities are. You know what is not safe. If you allow yourself to be pressured, things can turn out worse than if you stand up to the pressure.

I don't let directors or others on set make me do things my animals aren't prepared to do; that's the bottom line with me. I'd rather give up a job than go through the misery of the animal suffering and someone getting hurt. I certainly don't want my animals destroyed because I didn't step up to the plate, because that's usually the outcome. Somebody gets hurt, so the animal gets destroyed, when usually the animal is just doing what nature taught it to do and frequently acting out of fear.

I haven't had many confrontations about this, but do remember one time when I had a dog on set for a photo shoot for a cover for Woodward's Christmas catalogue. The photographer had to change film, so he said, "Okay, take a break but hold your spots," and he walked away from his camera. I was standing back from the shot but had the dog on a sit-stay. The make-up artist and the hairstylist moved in to tweak everybody up, and the hairstylist pulled out a can of hairspray to spray the model's hair. I went, "Whoa, wait a minute. You can't be doing that there."

"Why not?"

"Because the dog is sitting there."

"So?"

"That stuff will make the dog sick." Any kind of aerosol will make dogs vomit. So I said, "Take your model someplace else to do the spraying, okay?" To which she replied, "No. You take your dog out." I said, "It's harder to get the dog to hold its mark than it is a human, so better to keep the dog on its spot and take the person out." This dog was also a Dalmatian, and they can be pretty jittery.

Just then the photographer came in and he said, "Gary, you're wasting our time, and blah blah blah." He was giving me a rough time about this, and I finally said, "You know what? Either you do it my way, or the dog walks and you can do this shoot without a dog, because I'm not allowing my dog to get sick because of your stupidity." I was really mad. "On top of that, when I leave, I'll make a complaint to the SPCA about cruelty to animals on this set. You think Woodward's is going to like that?"

He said, "Your point is made. Okay, take the model out."

But you've got to do that, you know? You can't just turn a blind eye to stuff like that. These animals are working for us. Everyone is making money off these animals, and they deserve proper treatment. The animals I'm working with can't speak for themselves, so it's my job to speak for them.

"Bird on a Wire" was a great break for me, and the money provided a good pad in the beginning, but there weren't a lot of those kinds of gigs around. I soon learned that if I only pursued jobs as a wrangler, or as an animal agent for feature films, I'd starve to death. The old survival instinct kicked in, but this time, I wasn't prepared to put Cinemazoo aside and go out selling art supplies or something like that. I was determined to make Cinemazoo a success. There had to be another way of making money working with animals.

Want to see some of Gary's animal superstars?

http://cinemazoo.com/clientgallery.html

24 Surviving

Pet-sitting. Why not? It wasn't showbiz, but it was definitely about animals. However, if I was going to provide a pet-sitting service, it was going to be on a scale that would support the zoo I was building. I wasn't about to hire myself out as a pet-sitter. So I contracted people to be pet-sitters in 28 areas of the Lower Mainland (an area that includes Vancouver and all its surrounding communities). I made a deal with them. I said for a percentage of their fee, we'd do all the coordinating and administration for them. I'd have flyers made advertising their services that they could distribute in their community. When someone called to find out more, we'd take care of negotiating the fee and setting up the pet-sitting schedule. The pet-sitters thought it was a good deal, and we were in business!

It worked well, and the pet-sitting business did the job in terms of paying the bread and butter bills—covering the lean times between the more lucrative jobs acting as an agent and wrangler for films. Anyone who works in the field of animals knows it's a struggle to make a living this way. You're always on the edge of going out of business: that's why it's so competitive, you have to think on your feet to come up with ways to stay in there. The jobs that pay well are few and far between. You can make a lot of money one day, and then starve for the next six months—unless you've got some other kind of financial support, like a rich family.

My family—at least, my immediate family—was not rich. My parents gave me whatever support they could, but they didn't have money to spare. I started this business with an idea, a camera and a cat . . . and my own determination. That's it. I've had some good paying gigs, but otherwise, it's been pretty hand-to-mouth. I joke that when I left the Pacific Artists Studio—which I did in 1991—I went from being a starving artist to being animal poor.

Of course, I don't always make the wisest financial decisions. There have been times I haven't been able to pay the rent, but I'd go out and spend a couple of hundred dollars on a chameleon because I just knew I had to have it. I always think to myself, "Something is just around the corner that will save me," and it usually does.

I've also had a lot of great people who've given me support over the years. I have one friend, for instance: Cherry, an American friend, came to visit me one time. The morning after she left, I was sitting at my desk and opened my drawer to get something out and there was $3,000 US sitting in the drawer. I knew it came from her. I called her and said, "You know, Cherry, I can't take that money. I just can't, because I have no idea when I would ever be able to pay it back." She said, "Who said it was a loan? Have you never heard of anyone making a donation to an animal organization? I don't want to see you fall short. The animals will suffer. Consider it a donation for the animals."

Anyway, back to pet-sitting. It served its purpose; it helped pay the bills for several years. I gave it up after an incident when a pet went missing. Although we found the pet, the event was like a splash of cold water because I realized that if anything went wrong, it wasn't the pet-sitters that would be liable, it would be my company.

I spent two years at the Hamilton Street location, and then the owners of the building came to me and told me I had to move because the building was being expropriated for the province's utility company, BC Hydro. They said they had space in another building a block away on Homer Street, and that's where the zoo went next. It was actually a better space for the zoo, so not a sacrifice at all in that sense. However, I still had a few commercial artists renting space at the Hamilton office, so the move acted as a catalyst to make the break with the Pacific Artists Studios. It was difficult to do because of course it was never just a business—

I had longstanding relationships with many of the artists. I mean, the stories continued into the Hamilton location, albeit with new twists.

There was this one guy, a graphic artist, who had an office down the hallway from me. He worked a lot of late nights, and this one time I had a tiger on site because we were working a tiger for a job and the owner had left it with me. That tiger was absolutely dog-tame, a really friendly cat.

So this one night, I'm there and the building is dark except for the light coming out of this guy's office down the hall, which you could see because he's left the door open. I say to whoever I was with: "Let's let the tiger wander down the hallway here and see what he does."

So this tiger starts to walk down the hall. All the doors are closed except for the guy's at the end, so we watch the tiger make his way down the hall until he gets to this guy's office, where he stops because the light is attracting him. He's just standing there looking in, but of course he's a big animal and you can hear him breathing. All of a sudden, we hear: "Oh my God!" We hear banging and crashing and everything and we're wondering what's going on because we can see the back of the tiger still sticking out of the office, so we know the tiger isn't doing anything. Anyway, we run down to see what all the noise is about and when we look in the office the guy is standing on top of his filing cabinet. He's just shaking in his boots; he's terrified.

Well, of course we got him down and explained that the tiger was truly not dangerous; he was like a big domestic cat. I mean, I'd slept with that cat, I knew what it was like. But the poor guy said, "I thought I was in a bad dream." He couldn't believe it was happening. He said, "You're working there and you hear this breathing and you turn around and here's this 400-pound tiger standing there looking at you. It scared the pants off me." He wasn't mad, though. He said, "I have to admit, I've never had an experience like that before. How many guys could say that they had a tiger breathing down their neck while they were working?"

So, it was funny, but that was in my early wrangling days. Would I do it today? No, I wouldn't. It was a stupid thing to do and I was lucky that nothing bad happened. Look what happened with Siegfried and Roy. Roy Horn never thought one of his tigers would turn on him like that. So, no . . . but it sure did give me a laugh at the time.

We lasted two more years in Vancouver's Gastown area. Over that time, I continued to pay the rent through income from the pet-sitting service and through work on the occasional short film or lower-budget feature (the non-union films). Then one day, the landlord told me there was going to be a rent increase and gave me a letter that spelled out the details. I looked at the letter and just about fell to the floor. The increase would be almost three times what I was currently paying! Commercial real estate had begun to take off in that area and the owners felt they could get more than they were currently getting for their space.

There was no way I could afford to pay that kind of rent, so I began looking for another place; this time away from the downtown core. Not long after, I was driving along Hastings Street in east Vancouver on my way somewhere and I saw a big "For Lease" sign on a building. I went in and learned that it was a big basement space. There was a room that I thought would make a great space for some of the zoo animals, and a big empty space where I thought I could start a doggie daycare. I spoke with the landlord and learned that there was more space available on the second floor, so I took that as well and made the move to Burnaby. I moved most of the animals and my offices upstairs into the second floor—not an ideal space, because it was basically a bunch of small offices, about 12 by 12 feet apiece. I began with three of them and then kept renting more as I kept adding animals until I had nine.

I was there for ten years.

I was there without Tracy, because by then we'd decided to call it quits. It was all very friendly, but then everything between us was like that. We never fought, we never argued, we never had any disagreements. In all the years that we were together, we never had a problem, but to be honest: whatever the ingredient is that makes a deep, loving man-woman relationship, it wasn't there with us. We loved each other a lot, but like brother and sister. So when I decided to move the zoo to Burnaby, she decided that was a good time to make the break. She said, "You've got too much going on in your life. Cinemazoo is really taking off, and I think you need to concentrate on that." She'd been there at the beginning of Cinemazoo, and she continued to be supportive. I said, "I think you're right," and we separated.

Soon after, I met this incredible woman, Jane. Jane and I hit it off big time right from the start and, not surprisingly, knowing me, it wasn't too long until we moved in together. We were together for four incredible years. We had lots of fun and I've got great memories of our times together. One of the reasons I value the ring that the artists made for my 40th birthday is because Jane used to sleep with it because it reminded her of me. She put some pretty good birthday parties together for me herself.

But there were problems, and it came to a head one day when I returned home from work and she was talking to someone on the phone. She was upstairs, but she had a loud voice, and I heard her say, "Yeah, I guess I love Gary, but he's such a waste of time with that Cinemazoo. He's never going to amount to anything. You know, I can't stick with someone who's got those kinds of pipe dreams." It was like being stabbed in the back. When she came downstairs I just said, "Jane, it's over," and walked out. We're friends again now, have been for years, but I sure was angry with her then. I'm still friends with Tracy, too. In fact, I've remained friends with most of the women who've been part of my life.

Anyway, when I moved into the Burnaby space, I made one of the offices on the third floor into a bedroom for me.

I didn't figure I could afford to keep a room for my photography, but I worked out a deal with a couple who did wildlife photography that they could use the space for free if they occasionally let me use the studio myself for my own animal photography, and if they paid me for any of my animals they wanted to use in their shots. It was a good deal. For one thing, it turned out that they were two of Canada's leading wildlife photographers, Tom Kitchin and Victoria Hurst. Tom and Victoria have had their work in all kinds of publications, like Field & Stream, Newsweek, Time and Reader's Digest. A couple of years ago they did all the photographs of the big cats in the book, "Forest Cats of North America."

I learned so much about wildlife photography from Tom and Victoria, and have an enormous respect for their work, like their photography done on safaris. You know people have this image of wildlife photographers being out in the wild, sitting for long periods of time hidden behind blinds waiting for the right shot. Tom and Victoria certainly did shoots in safaris and in the wild, but much of their work was done in studio or in nature using trained animals.

Tom and Vicky had taken tons of beautiful wolf pictures, and I remember my surprise when I found out that all the wolves were trained. Sometimes when a hunt scene was involved, they would release a partridge or something of that nature, and a lynx would come out of the tree and capture it so that it could all be caught on film. It was actually a really good use of the animals because it was stimulating for them, much better than sitting around in a cage. It helped to maintain their wildness. At the end of the day, though, the trainer would blow his or her whistle and the animals would come back and be taken home. The shots were amazing, though, just amazing, because they had more control. And, of course, they were able to set up something in a day that might take months to get in the wild.

They used many of my animals in studio shots, and I learned by helping them set up my animals and by asking questions. There's a great photo of one of my rattlesnakes that appeared in an edition of Beautiful BC where the snake is seen on the desert floor with a blue sky above. That shot was done with the rattle-snake on a tabletop. I have photos of me manipulating the snake and getting it into position.

The other thing about this place in Burnaby was that it was located within a block of a huge undeveloped park area right on the east end of Burnaby. There were actually wild animals there. I could get up early in the morning and walk outside and there would be deer grazing at the edge of the building. The first pileated woodpecker I ever saw was one that used to hang around there all the time. A coyote almost ran into me one day as it came around the corner of a building while I was sitting on a retainer wall there. Scared us both. Blackberries grew wild all over, which was great because a lot of the insects I was raising—like the walking sticks and the leaf bugs—survived on blackberry leaves. All I had to do was walk outside to get their food source.

The only real problem was having to keep my animals in all those different little rooms, but I figured it was worth that sacrifice for the rest, especially for the space in the basement that was going to allow me to get the dog daycare up and running. To me, it made more sense for people to bring their pets to us, rather than having to manage a raft of pet-sitters and the scheduling issues that came with that. Also, while I would still be liable for any harm an animal might come to under my care, having them in my own space meant I could be sure of the care they were getting. The chance of any mishap was greatly reduced.

Having a dog daycare was something I'd wanted to do

for some time, ever since a friend had sent me a newspaper clipping about this woman in Chicago who'd started that kind of thing there. Dog daycares are common today, but they were unknown at the time, and when I first heard about it, no one else was doing it in Vancouver. I thought it was just a great idea, but I'd never had the space when I was renting the Gastown offices. Now I did.

Ironically, many of my clients came from the one person who had opened a dog daycare business in the intervening time, and turned out to provide a shoddy service. I won't go into detail . . . let's just say his methods were a bit questionable. I think it says a lot that one of my customers was his landlady. She had three dogs and wouldn't take them to him because of the way he treated the animals in his care. His own staff finally reported him. They didn't want to work for a person who did those kinds of things. I mean, the guy was a bit strange. One time, all our sandwich boards in front of our building disappeared, and his staff told me he'd taken them; another case of competition paranoia. Anyway, the last I heard of him, he'd left town. The people who worked for him continued the business and we had no more problems. In fact, we got really busy, and they did well too.

I had the daycare for many years—most of the time that we were in that location—but in the end I sold it to the woman who'd been running it for me. But you know, although I knew it was time for me to move on from that kind of business, the pet-sitting and the dog daycare gave me a reservoir of animals to sign up for my agency. All of those kinds of things I was doing were helping me to learn more about the different varieties of animals; it was all good knowledge and experience.

During those years, I'd begun to take Cinemazoo into new directions. I had begun taking my animals to school classrooms, where I would talk with the kids about the animals and about conservation. I'd also started doing this at the BC Burnaby Correctional Centre for youth in the jail there. I was being asked to appear on talk shows, and I'd been getting a lot more work doing things like commercials and shoots for magazine ads, even acting as agent and wrangler for animals in music videos. In fact, I supplied a wolf for Shania Twain's first CD cover.

But the gigs that paid best were handling animals used for special presentations at corporate conventions and other public events. Some of my best memories come from those gigs.

25 Animal Crackers

When I was small, I used to think the big animal adventures happened out in the wild—you know, Jim on "Wild Kingdom"—but some of my biggest adventures have happened at business conventions. Who'da thunk, eh?

I remember once being hired by a company to do an appearance at their convention. They asked me to wear a three-piece business suit and carry an attaché case and to bring a tiger to the event. Their plan was to show a promotional film to an assembled crowd of about 400, and then at the end of the film, the lights would all go down and a spotlight would focus on the back door of the theatre. I was to enter, holding the tiger and the attaché case, and walk down the aisle to the stage while the music "Eye of the Tiger" was played. I thought this would be pretty cool and I was looking forward to it.

Well, I'm standing out there in the hall with the tiger, waiting to come in. Now, this is the same tiger that I wrote about before—a big pussycat. This cat really loved me, and whenever it was near me, it wanted to hug me all the time and to play. So we're waiting out there, and I'm looking through the crack in the door and just thinking it's time to take hold of the tiger to get ready for our walk-on, when the tiger comes up behind me and swipes my feet right out from under me and pounces on me and holds me down. Playtime, in her mind. The trainer tries to get her off but she won't budge. This is a big cat.

I figured the only thing I could do was not react, just freeze, and she'd get bored. So I didn't move and sure enough, she started to move off. I began to get up, and wham, she pounced right back on me. It was kind of like she was playing with a mouse and I was it. So I just made sure I didn't move until she got right back up and the trainer grabbed her. I got up, straightened myself and grabbed the attaché case and the leash and right then, the doors opened and in we walked and everything else went fine. She walked down the aisle slowly, looking left to right; we got to the stage and stood there and everyone applauded. It was great. But I was thinking that if they'd opened the doors one minute earlier, they'd have seen this big terrifying tiger laying on me licking my face.

I always like it when the situation calls for a bit of drama, of pizzazz—when I have to assume some kind of persona, put on a bit of theatre. Which is interesting, because when you meet me, I'm not at all theatrical. I wear a big black cowboy hat, but that's because I'm bald and I like cowboy hats. Otherwise, I'm kind of laid back. I guess being in these shows provides an outlet for that more theatrical part of me.

Anyway, you'll understand why the following "performance" stands out in my mind.

It was a fiftieth birthday party like no other I've been to, put on at the Westin Bayshore Hotel (one of the most expensive hotels in Vancouver). The fellow who was turning 50 owned a very large corporation in town. It was a very fancy affair, all black-tie.

They wanted me and another handler to come in and walk around the tables set up in the ballroom holding eagles. So that is what we did. I had a golden eagle and my friend James had a bald eagle. First we walked around the tables with these huge eagles on our fists, and then we left. After a short period of time, we entered again and went and stood in a corner of the ballroom. People would come over and talk to us about the birds and about handling them. After awhile, we left for another break.

Then they called us in back in, and this was the part that was really spectacular. They asked us to stand at the head table where this guy Billy, whose birthday it was, was sitting with his brothers and sisters and the rest of his family. We were told to stand about six feet apart and to face the back of the ballroom. Our backs were to Billy and the rest of the head table.

We stood there immobile until we heard our cue—the music "Born to be Wild"—and then, with spotlights focused on us, we raised the eagles up in the air. Now if you just tilt your hand a bit, eagles try to get their balance by spreading their wings out, and you can keep their wings out by keeping your hand tilted.

So there we are with the eagles above us with their wings spread out, and the music becomes, louder and then all of a sudden, we hear this loud sound from out in the lobby: "Vroom! Vroom!" The doors open up and this guy on a Harley is out there, dressed like the Chinese guy with the bowler hat and tails in the 007 movies. He rides this bike—a 100th Anniversary Limited Edition Harley—right up to the head table and they present this bike to the birthday guy. It's his birthday present. It's a pretty spectacular performance, all in all.

One of the great things about doing these events is that you never know what kind of animal they're going to want. I've had to work with all manner of big cats, and even with goats.

That was also at the Bayshore. It was a Greek wedding and very formal—everyone was in tux and gowns. I had to dress up like a herdsman and lead in a bunch of goats that were intended to be symbolic of the bride's dowry. But as soon as I got the goats onto the hardwood floor in the reception hall, the goats started pooping. So there I was on my hands and knees, with a little scoop, scooping up the poops as we went along. I was crawling through this reception hall full of gorgeous people, so what else could I do? I just kept lifting the tray up, offering "Raisin rosettes?" They were great. They all laughed.

I mean, I've had to walk into conventions with every kind of animal.

One time, I had to do this gig for a stock market company whose logo was an alligator and a bull. They were having a celebration at a local restaurant called Umberto's, and I was supposed to do a walk-through holding an alligator while another guy led a bull.

Well, first off, I couldn't get a bull in time, so I had this huge ox; and instead of an alligator I used my five-foot caiman. The caiman was no problem, but the ox was really huge—it's one that is often seen at the PNE. It's a giant.

This particular Umberto's restaurant has a large brick-walled courtyard, and there is an entryway to the courtyard leading from a rather narrow alley—more of a big pathway—that leads from the actual alley. We have to bring the ox in from the alley and then down that pathway to the courtyard, where it will be put into an iron pen put in the courtyard for that purpose.

I think, "Hmmmmm. This might be a little narrow for him to go down," but we figure we'll try it anyway. So we get the ox from the alley into the pathway leading to the courtyard, but as soon as we get him in there, the guy who's supposed to lead him discovers he doesn't want to be in front of the ox because if it bolts, he'll be trampled. So I suggest we let it go on its own and herd it from behind.

Well, that thing felt the wall on each side of it and panicked. I could see this ox going right through the courtyard and into the adjoining restaurant. I thought, "Oh my God, I'm doomed." The ox entered the courtyard and had two choices—go into the pen or go into the restaurant. Fortunately, the ox chose the pen. That was one scary moment, I'll tell you.

We got the gate closed and then I went and got the alligator and just stood there by the pen holding it for the whole day. From that point on, it was a very uneventful day.

The only other time when I think I've been truly worried about public safety during a performance was a time when I supplied a jaguar for an event and it ran amok.

In that case, I wasn't handling the cat: the owner was, and the guy decided to do a bit of showboating. He'd been showing the jaguar to a large crowd at a club, and instead of having the cage brought to the animal at the end of the show—which is what you should do—he got one of his people to clear a path through the crowd with the intention of walking the jaguar through the it and out the back door. Except as they started this walk, something spooked the jaguar and he went crazy and began running in all directions.

I was standing in front of the front door preventing people from coming in, saying, "Stay back. Stay back," waiting for the guy to get his cat under control. But the cat was running around and people were scrambling all over the place. There were a couple of liquor bars in the club and they were jumping over them. One guy actually fell over the bar. The poor jaguar was just trying to find an escape route.

Finally, the cat started heading for the front door where I was standing. I was thinking "Oh my God," because if she got past me and the people outside, she'd split and could run out onto Granville Street, one of Vancouver's main downtown streets. We sure didn't need a jaguar running loose in the busy downtown area.

Then she started running right for me. Now, I had worked with that jaguar in the past and she knew me really well. One of the things she used to do was come up and set her head on my lap. It loved having her head in my lap while I scratched her neck. However, that was when she was a year old; this was 13 years later. I had no idea if she even remembered me. But she ran up to me and then just jammed her head right in between my legs, and as soon as she did that, she just laid down and stayed there. I squatted and started scratching her back and she was panting away.

Her owner came, and I got the chain hooked up to her and gave it back to him. I was seething as I told the guy: "Put her back on the platform. Bring the cage in. Put her in the cage and take her out that way." I was very angry with this guy, because he was a professional and should have known better. I knew this guy. He was a good wrangler and he knew what the rules were when you're working with a dangerous exotic animal. I guess he relearned a lesson that day.

Horses are fun, though. I've probably had more opportunity than anyone on the planet to bring horses into hotels. In Vancouver, I've led horses through the Four Seasons, the Hotel Vancouver, the Sheraton and the Bayshore. And I—or perhaps I should say they—haven't had an accident of the rosette variety yet, even though I've had to take them up freight elevators and they've had to walk into crowded ballrooms carrying unfamiliar and inexperienced riders (important persons from whatever company was hosting the event, usually).

But believe it or not, the gigs that have brought the greatest financial return have been those involving sheep. Two of these jobs stand out in my mind. One happened here in Vancouver, where I had to supply three sheep for a Woodward's wool catalogue shoot and Danine and I ended up getting our photo on the front page of one of the big dailies. There we were, walking these sheep through the streets of downtown Vancouver. The story was syndicated in papers across the country, so I had friends calling from the east saying, "Hey, you're in our newspaper!" My mom said she always knew I'd be famous, but not for walking a sheep in the middle of a city.

The other job resulted from a call from someone in New York representing the Australian Woolmark company. They wanted to know if I could come to New York and wrangle some sheep for an ad for the company. They offered me an unheard-of fee: $19,000 US. I thought, "This is too good to be true." They asked if I had sheep in New York. I said, "Sure. Sure." I didn't, but I knew I could find some. I never think I can't do something.

I called the head office of the 4-H Sheep Clubs in Washington, D.C. and asked for a list of 4-H sheep farms in upstate New York. The very first place I called, the people said that yes, they had two sheep and they were halter-trained, which meant they could walk through something like a county fair and not even blink. That was perfect, just what I needed. I asked if they could send me photos, which they did. I sent the photos to the client and he liked them. It was a done deal.

The sheep owners thought I'd need time to train the sheep to do what I needed them to do, so I arrived in New York five days early. As it turned out, I didn't need five minutes. The first time we took them out, I took them down to a highway with lots of traffic. They walked by the traffic no problem. We banged garbage lids; we tried all kinds of things. Nothing fazed them. They'd just kind of look over and keep going.

These people were super. They even offered to put me up for a few days, saying, "Why stay in a hotel if you've got to keep coming back and forth to work with the sheep?" The guy had a week off, and he took me sightseeing. I saw the Statue of Liberty, the Empire State Building, Central Park and even some of the famous mansions. We had a great time.

The day before the shoot, I met with the production team. After making sure that I had a staff with a hook on the end so that I could pull the sheep back if they started to stray, the director said, "Here's the scenario. Two supermodels from the Ford Modeling Agency will be walking the sheep. You're going to be about 12 feet back, just making sure everything goes okay. The models will be hand-ing out calling cards, so every now and then you can go up and hand them more. Okay?" I said, "That's fine."

So we met at the office in the morning. They put on a beautiful big breakfast spread and I had a great meal while the girls were getting their suits on and their make-up done. I was dressed in one of those Australian oilskin coats with the flap on the back. Then the director told us that the first place on our agenda was the Morning Show.

The station wasn't far from the company's office, so we walked the sheep there. We arrive and there were all these people standing outside waiting to see the show. The models, holding the sheep, joined the line. After awhile Al, the weatherman for the show, came out holding a hand-mic and began interviewing people for the show. Our plan, of course, was that he interview our models, who would tell him about the product.

My director suggests it might be a good idea for me to go and stand beside the sheep and make sure that they don't make a distraction while the girls are talking about the wool. I say, "No problem," and go to join the girls and the sheep.

So I'm standing there with the models and the sheep and sure enough, Al comes up with his microphone. The first thing he says is, "So, what are these sheep all about?" I can see the monitors, and can see that the cameras are focused on the sheep, not the girls. The models are saying, "Well, we're here to promote Australian Woolmark, and that wool is a fabric that can be worn all year round, and blah, blah, blah." They're trying to get the company's message across. But Al kind of cuts them off. He says, "That's great, girls," and then he holds the mic over to me and the cameras all shift to me. Al asks, "Are you the sheep herder?" I say, "No, actually I'm the sheeps' agent." He hesitates. This obviously intrigues him.

"These sheep have an agent?"

"Yeah."

"You're their agent."

"Um. Yeah."

"What's your company?"

"Cinemazoo Animal Agency."

"Do I want to know how much these sheep are making?"

"You might not."

"Right. That could really get me upset if I found out it was more than I make." Then he says, "What's your name?" And I tell him.

"Where are you from?"

"Vancouver."

"Vancouver, Washington?"

"No. Vancouver, British Columbia."

"Do you mean to tell me we don't have any sheep here in the United States?"

"No, I'm from British Columbia. The sheep are from upstate New York. They're New York sheep. "

"Oh, that's good," he says. "Are they nice sheep?"

I say, "Yeah, feel the wool," and I start hamming it up a bit, talking about the wool. I don't know what to do.

So he goes, "Yeah, nice wool," and then he turns it back to the studio saying they have breaking news or whatever. Then he turns back to me and asks if I'd be willing to come in and do a bit of talk on the show about what I do. "We've never had anybody like you on before." I say sure, but that I would need to check with my director, who also says sure. He says I should go in and talk about the work I'm doing for the company, Australian Woolmark. He sees it as an opportunity to get more publicity.

So they lead me to the green room to wait. There's a couch in there with a guy sitting on it reading a paper, and a big easy chair, plus a coffee table filled with all kinds of cookies and pastries, muffins, juices and coffee. "Help yourself," they say, "We'll be with you in a few minutes."

So I pick up a cookie and sit down on the couch. The guy reading the newspaper puts it down and I see it's Elton John! I go, "It's you!" Duh. I don't know what else to say.

He said, "Yeah, it's me," then he went on in a conversational tone: "I've been here for a while. How about you?" So we got talking. He asked what I was doing there, and so I told him a bit about me and what I do. He said he remembered coming to Vancouver, B.C. one time to perform, and I said, "Yeah, I photographed you that time. I was working as a photographer for an interviewer and she did the interview with you in your dressing room." He said, "I hope you won't be offended if I tell you I don't remember you." I said, "No, you look a lot different now, too. I only remember you because you're Elton John."

So we laughed and kept on talking, and then the director came in and said they weren't going to be able to get me on the show. They thanked me and gave me a t-shirt and promised to send a clip of the interview shot outside.

So I went back out and told my guys that I wouldn't be on. The director said that was okay, that they'd come up with a new plan. I had this big Australian oilskin coat on with big pockets, so he said they'd stuff my pockets full of these calling cards we were giving out, and I'd walk the sheep while the girls would walk on either side of me holding onto my arm and handing out the cards. He said, "People have already seen you. They haven't seen the girls."

So we walked about a block and this lady came up: "Oh, hi, how are you?" I went, "Fine." She said, "Are you a movie star?"

"No."

"Those sheep are wonderful, they're so cute. Are you sure you're not a movie star? You look like one on TV."

On TV? How could she have seen it on TV when it happened just minutes ago and we were in the middle of downtown New York? So I asked her, and she said, "Oh, you were projected 16 storeys high on the Videotron in Times Square."

"I was on that?"

"Yes."

The only time I'd ever seen that was on the televised New Years Eve celebration from Times Square. "Cool."

The rest of our walk through New York was uneventful, except that people were always coming up and making a fuss over the sheep. The director said, "I have never seen New Yorkers so friendly in my life." It was a lot of fun. I had such a ball that day. I was sad when it was over. I was flying back and thinking, "Wow, I just met Elton John. I walked down the streets of New York with two beautiful supermodels on my arms, and I got paid $19,000 US to boot. Hello! Am I dreaming?"

To see what Gary does in the classroom, visit:

http://www.savingcinemazoo.com/episode3.html

26 On a More Serious Note

All of that stuff was fun. Some of it even made me a fair amount of money, but it was all supporting what was quickly becoming the driving force of Cinemazoo: the desire to create greater public awareness of and care for these animals.

A couple of years after I'd moved the zoo to Burnaby, I received a request from the teacher of a kid that I knew: to bring some of my animals to her classroom for the kids to see. I was happy to do that, and it went well. I just brought out the animals and held each one up and talked about it. The kids asked questions and were able to touch the animals. The teacher said, "Oh, this is wonderful. I know other teachers would like to have you come to their class as well." She started passing my name around, and we started getting more and more work doing classroom presentations. In addition to being personally rewarding, it ended up providing good financial support for the zoo.

Then the government got wind of what I was doing and asked me if I could do a presentation at the Burnaby Youth Detention Centre. I did one, and they kept bringing me back. Finally they gave me a contract to provide regular presentations to the youth there. They even kept on Cinemazoo when other programs were being cut back due to restricted budgets. In fact, they told me that when it came to deciding what programs to keep, Cinemazoo was the first choice. I was very pleased and proud to know that we were thought of so highly. I still do presentations there. At that time I was doing 10 per year; now I'm contracted to do 16.

I love doing this work. I really do. I remember when I was a kid and this guy came to show us his collection of stuffed owls. I was enthralled. I talked about him for days. I'm thrilled to think I might be this guy for some of the kids I'm talking with in the schools and in the jail. I know that when I'm talking about animals, the kids know that what I'm talking about is something that I love. If I can inspire one kid to become an animal enthusiast, maybe even a conservationist, it'll be worth it. Who knows? That kid could end up being responsible for saving an endangered species!

Of course, there's a difference between the presentations in the schools and the one I do at the jail. In the school classroom, we talk first and foremost about the animals. When I go to the penitentiary, we talk on a more personal level. I talk about what I did as a kid, what I did growing up and the things that I've learned that I've been able to put in practice—specifically how I've been able to make a career of it and earn an income. I usually say, "You know, you guys, most of you are in here for assault or firearm infractions, or stealing cars and racing them and then smashing them up, stuff like that. Here's the thing: if you could take what you've learned about doing that stuff and put it to practice working in the film industry, you could actually make a good living doing that. If you're athletic, or artistic, or good with electronics, same thing. There's work in special effects. If you could learn how to control your fighting so that it looks real but no one gets hurt, you could work as a stuntman. Those guys make good money. If you're interested, let me know. I'll give you names of stunt schools and maybe you can get sponsored through the career courses here at the correctional institute."

I'm always hoping that when I'm doing presentations, I'm making a difference to a kid, that I'm opening his or her eyes to a whole new world. And, of course, there's always my grandfather over my shoulder urging me on.

The other thing we did in Burnaby was to open up nature clubs for kids. They went on film trips, they did crafts based on the subject of the day, there were guest speakers, and the kids got to help feed the animals and clean their cages. I had an awesome instructor, Dawn Saunders, who also taught at a childcare centre. She was great with the kids, loved animals, loved doing crafts—it all fit in really nicely. Never a money-maker, though, because the fee to join was low, and then once I paid the instructor there was not much left over. But that wasn't the point. It was so kids could share in the enjoyment of working with and learning about animals.

Sometimes I see these kids again, often when they're much older. I'll be walking down the street and one will see me and come over. "Hey, you're the guy that came to see us." And then he'll talk about what that meant for him. "Yeah, it was the greatest show we ever had." It makes me feel very good to hear that.

You know, when I think about how my love for animals affected my life . . . I didn't have time for drugs, or doing criminal activities or hanging around. I never spent a lot of time wondering what I wanted to do in my life. I couldn't always make it happen, but because of animals, I always had a focus. I had a dream. And I was never idle.

I tell people—kids, adults, whatever—that because of animals, I've had more adventures and met more people than I would have ever thought possible. I've even met Jane Goodall! Now *that* was really cool.

This woman called and told me she had a capuchin monkey—you know, the monkeys usually associated with organ grinders. The monkey had been her husband's and had only related to him. Her husband had died and now she could do nothing with the monkey. It hated her. She'd tried to give it away to others, but it always grabbed the bars and started shaking and screaming at the people. She was at her wit's end. She asked if I could come and see the monkey and maybe take him away.

Perhaps I looked like her husband or something, but when I came in this monkey—whose name was Gilly—was very calm.

I've learned that if you approach an animal—especially a wild animal—wanting to be their friend right away, it can be intimidating for the animal. This is true especially if you're looking right at them, because with some animals, that's taken as a threat. I saw this in action with a pack of wolves where the alpha wolf would take on each of the wolves and put them in their place. I was advised, "Don't look at the wolf. Don't look at her at all, because she will think that you're challenging her next." I just went on working on the set, ignoring her. I had some wieners in my pocket that I'd break up and throw on the ground close to her, but otherwise I'd just keep going on with my business. Pretty soon she realized I wasn't a threat.

With this monkey, I did basically the same thing. I ignored him. I talked with the lady. I walked over to the library, opened some books and pretended I was reading. Then I went and sat down beside the cage and said, 'Do you have any grapes or fruit?" She said, "Yes, I'll get you some." So she brought them to me and I sat there and the monkey was watching me the whole time while I was eating these grapes. Out of the corner of my eye, I could see the monkey reaching his hand through the bars, wanting a grape, so very nonchalantly I put a grape in his hand and kept on eating myself. He ate that grape and then reached through the cage for another. This time I shifted my chair over really close to the cage and handed him another grape. Then I laid my arm near the bottom of the cage and Gilly came down and began grooming the hair on my arm. The woman said, "That's it. He's yours. You're the first person he's ever reacted to like that."

So I took Gilly back to Cinemazoo. He was fine with me; in fact, he'd groom me for hours. It used to freak me out a bit because he'd be grooming my arm and every now and then he'd come up with something, look at it, and put it in his mouth. I'd go, "Just what did you find?" But he wouldn't come out of his cage, and between groomings, he was still an unhappy monkey.

There was always a fair amount of activity in Cinemazoo, and he eventually calmed down around other people; like, I had a couple of people working for me then, and they got to be friendly with Gilly. I was thinking things were getting better, until one day when I was at home and got a phone call from one of my staff: "Gary, I'm in the hospital. Gilly bit me. I'm getting stitches." This happened again, and I had to face the fact that Gilly was a liability. What to do?

Coincidentally, right at that time Jane Goodall was in town doing a lecture at the Trade and Convention Centre. So I went there to hear her speak. I waited until after the lecture was over, and I got an opportunity to talk with her. I told her about Gilly. I said, "The animal has never been out of his cage. I've opened the door, he refuses to come out." I told her that it saddened me because it seemed there was fear in his heart. She offered to come down and have a look at Gilly, which was terrific. I mean, Jane Goodall is one of my heroes. I was absolutely thrilled that she would come to Cinemazoo.

The next morning she arrived. She had a look at Gilly and we talked. I said I just didn't know what to do with him, but I knew this was no life for a primate. They need more space to move around. If Gilly would come out of his cage, he could travel with me and get stimulation that way, but staying in his cage 24/7 was not right for him or any animal that needs movement.

Jane gave me the name of a place in Texas that rehabilitates primates—gets them ready to go back into nature. They had the right facilities and could provide the right care. So I thought, "Well, okay, that's great." In the meantime, I really needed to get this little guy out of my building so nobody got hurt.

A few days later, a fellow came along who claimed he knew a lot about primates and he and Gilly clicked, just like that. He wanted Gilly. I said, "Well, if keeping Gilly doesn't work out for you, are you willing to share the expense of sending Gilly to this rehabilitation centre?" He said, "Definitely," but he continued, "I think he'll be happy with me." I gave Gilly to the guy, but when I learned he had a wife and a kid, I warned him not to let his child get too near Gilly because the monkey was unpredictable. He assured me that Gilly would be kept in a separate shed on his property that was heated. He'd be fine. He said, "We'll leave the door open all the time so eventually he'll come out."

Well, two months later, his wife brought Gilly back. He was in his cage in the back of a truck and the cage was covered. I said, "What's wrong"? She said, "It bit my husband and he doesn't want it anymore." She told me that her husband had been reaching into Gilly's cage to get something and Gilly attacked. I said, "Oh. Okay, well is he willing to help me with the cost of shipping Gilly to Texas as he promised?" She said, "Well, I don't know. We've got a lot of medical expenses. He had to have reconstructive surgery on his arm because Gilly ripped him bad."

So, I ended up sending Gilly to Texas and paying for it myself. That was the last time I saw Gilly, so I hope it went well. There was sure something a bit deranged in that little guy's mind, a fear of some kind. Who knows? I mean when you're locked up all the time, it's like being in solitary confinement all your life, you know? Things could just snap. Primate's minds are similar to ours, only on a smaller scale. I wonder if Gilly might have had some kind of schizophrenia or was bipolar.

I know that we are careful to ensure that the animals that we have at Cinemazoo that are in cages get stimulation. We try to motivate them to move around, and we give them lots of toys to play with. Sometimes we make eating a challenge for them; like, we put food inside a dog's kong toy so they have to work to get at it. A lot of the animals that we have are animals that are sedentary. They stay in one place as long as the food is there. We've got a turtle that can sit in one spot for a year in the wild as long as it's got food sources passing by, because it lures its prey into its mouth. Some of the snakes will either go into a burrow or climb up into the fork of a tree once they've bagged their food, and they'll sit up there for weeks digesting their meal.

Some animals are only motivated to move for three reasons: hunting, eating and mating. Other than that, they conserve their energy, because the more they move about, the more they need to eat to rebuild and replenish their energy and their body weight. Reptiles, especially, can be very sedentary.

I'll have someone come into the zoo and see this 150-pound turtle sitting in this huge Rubbermaid cattle trough we have (it's six feet across). They'll say, "Well, that's not right, you know? It's not fair to the animal to have it stuck in a little thing like that." They don't realize that that animal in the wild doesn't move any more than it does here. They figure if it's in the wild, it's free and so will be moving, but animals like turtles don't move. If you were to look at the excrement of this turtle for example, it's almost a fine powder. When turtles eat, they use all the food that they have to keep their body weight, to keep their energy, and to keep them sustained over a long period of time, because they don't know when the next meal is coming. They're perfectly happy as long as they're fed.

But that's turtles. Other animals need to be stimulated more so that they don't get bored. Taking them out on presentations is one way of stimulating them. In fact, the animals I use in the presentations tend to be healthier than the others. It's good that people care about animals and that they keep their eyes open for animals that are being mistreated, but it's also good to know when it's actually mistreatment.

Let me give you another example.

I was asked to supply some chimpanzees for a Mattel toy commercial. I contacted some people in Santa Fe who had chimps, and they brought the chimps up for the shoot at the Lion's Gate Studios in North Vancouver. It was August and it was really hot. The chimps' owners had a big air-conditioned truck that held all the cages, food, everything—it was totally self-contained, but there were long stretches in between the scenes with the chimps.

You don't want to keep chimps in cages all day, so we'd take them out for walks frequently so they wouldn't get bored. They were on leashes—well, the leashes were more like loose necklaces—but they were trained to stay on them and the leashes were so long that while we walked along, the chimps would be playing in the grass and climbing trees and such. Actually, one of their favourite games was taking their hands and slapping them down on the tarmac to make a popping noise. They would run up to one another and make these popping noises and laugh and jump around. It was hilarious.

Later one day, we'd come back and we were all sitting around in the truck and the SPCA showed up. They said, "Are you Gary Oliver?" I said, "Yes."

"Are you the one in charge of these chimps?"

"Yes."

"We've had a complaint."

"A complaint from where? From who?"

"Somebody in one of the buildings here was watching you take the chimps for a walk and they have a complaint."

I couldn't imagine what there was to complain about. I asked, "What would be the complaint?" The guy said, "I almost feel dumb telling you this but we got the complaint so we have to follow up with it. The complaint is that you don't have shoes on the chimps."

"You've got to be kidding."

"No. That's the complaint."

I said, "Well, you know, they have shoes but they only wear them when they're on sets because they're not really very comfortable in them. We let them go natural whenever they can."

"Well, the complaint was about the chimps running on the tarmac without shoes." I said, "Do you agree with the complaint?" He said, "No, but I have to follow up with any complaint." I said, "Well, this person does not know what they're talking about, and if I did put shoes on them, you'd likely get ten more complaints from people who thought I was binding their feet and that it was unnatural."

He said, "Exactly," and put 'unfounded' on the report and said, "Don't worry about it."

But again, you know, I'd rather people care than not care, and some of their concern—even if uninformed—is understandable. Like how the animals are shipped. For instance, I actually get my tarantulas sent in the mail. They're wrapped up pretty tightly in little baggies in cotton batting and several of them can be included in a Styrofoam box and they can be two weeks in transit. Someone might think they wouldn't survive that, but in fact, tarantulas seem to know instinctively to shut down their body metabolism in that kind of situation. When they arrive and I open the box, they stretch their legs and away they go.

But, normally I don't buy animals. Nearly all our animals are rescued. People buy exotic pets and then can't (or no longer want to) take care of them, and they bring them in to Cinemazoo. Like Gilly. Gilly was a rescue animal. A rescue animal came in just yesterday—a red-eared slider turtle. This little green turtle is one of the most common rescued animals in the reptile world. People think they're so cute, but they grow to be big turtles that can bite. They don't do anything but sit and eat and poop, so people get bored with them. It's amazing how many species people have in their apartments, or their houses or their garages. I've been in this business for a long time now and so I'm getting known for rescuing animals. I know I just have to wait and people will bring me animals they no longer want to keep.

Now something people should be worried about is where these exotic animals are coming from. I'll take animals that have been captive-bred and I'll rescue animals that others have captured, but you'll never see me taking animals out of the wild, at least not knowingly.

I had a guy come in one time who said he was bringing in reptiles and selling them at wholesale prices. He said he went to California and chose the specimens he wanted and then had them shipped here. I said I was interested in buying some chameleons. He said he was bringing some in. But when I saw the shape they were in when they arrived, I though "Uh-uh, there's something wrong here." They were beautiful, but almost one third of them had died in shipment. That shouldn't happen. I noted the name of the company on a label on the box and took it upon myself to call the company to find out why that happened. I said, "Can I ask you a question? Are those captive-bred animals, or are they wild-caught?" He said, "No, they're wild-caught."

Well, when I had first talked to the guy selling the chameleons to me, I'd asked if they were wild-caught and he'd said no. So I went back to him and I said, "You lied to me. You told me these were captive-bred and I just found out that they're wild-caught. Take your animals away. I don't want any part of this."

Wild-caught animals should not be in cages, and if I know that I've rescued an animal that was originally in the wild, and I'm showing this animal to anyone, I point out that the animal was wild-caught and so hasn't been conditioned through breeding to be a captive animal, so it's harder on this animal to be in a cage than on a captive-bred animal. At least then it serves an educational purpose; plus, I'd rather have it where I know it's being taken care of and stimulated than unwanted and abandoned in someone's house.

With the exception of breeding for conservation purposes—say, to change the gene pool of a species suffering from inbreeding—I don't think in this day and age there is any need to capture animals in the wild. But I'm aware that this goes on: there are animals of every description you can think of that are being sold or bought or traded. I can at least provide a place of rescue, a place where they can get the best treatment with knowledgeable people. If there's a possibility of rehabilitating them back to the wild, like we were able to do with Gilly, I want to be a part of that.

In the meantime, I'll continue to show my animals and raise awareness of this issue and try to help people understand these animals and their needs. Hopefully, one day, there will be far fewer animals that need to be rescued.

27 The Move to Surrey

I was doing a lot of interesting work, but the jobs that paid well were still too few and far between and I was spending too much money—not on foolish stuff, at least not in my mind, but on animals. And as I kept collecting animals, I kept increasing the number of rooms I had to rent, so the rent was getting out of hand.

I had a great landlord, a Chinese man who believed in me and in what I was doing, to the point where he let several months go by without me paying any rent. He said, "You're here all the time, you work hard, and you're passionate about what you're doing. I believe you're going to make it, so don't worry about the rent." I think it also suited him that I was living there, because it was like having built-in security for the building. Twice I saw fires developing in the building and reported them. One of those times I actually put the fire out. Another time I stopped a break-in from happening. I ended up owing him a huge amount of money, but he's never asked me for a penny of it and I don't think he actually expects to be paid back. I hope, though, that he knows that I do remember and that when things work out for me, one of the first things I'm going to do is pay him back.

However, he wasn't that happy about having the animals in the rooms, and finally even he said, "You've got to admit, Gary, that this is not the right location for you." And it wasn't. Not just because I couldn't afford it, but also because the space was so weird. People would come up to the second floor expecting to find offices and they'd open up a door and find tanks full of lizards or snakes or whatever. I mean, it was kind of humorous, but it was annoying at the same time because lots of those people would end up wanting a tour, and because I'm proud of my animals and like to talk about them, I'd spend much of my day taking people from office to office on tours. I did this for free, of course, so it was adding to my financial stress. And while my landlord was understanding, bottom line? He wasn't that happy about having all the animals in the rooms. So it was time to move.

I happened to be doing a presentation in Surrey, a community east of Vancouver and Burnaby. I saw this building with a "For Rent" sign in the window and I thought maybe it would do. I went in and checked it out. It was really disgusting inside and it looked like it hasn't been occupied for a while, but it was storefront and street-level, so we could make the zoo open to the public. It would even be accessible for people in wheelchairs. I had heard a few negative things about the area, but it didn't look too bad the day I was there, and there was lots of space for the zoo plus a room upstairs where I could bunk. I talked to the owner and the price was right, so I thought, "Why not?" In 2000, we made the move to Surrey.

Cinemazoo has continued to expand. The list of film and television shows using animals I supply has grown and now includes films like "Look Who's Talking Now," "Sisterhood," "101 Dalmations," "Snakes on a Plane," and the "Police Academy" series. I was hired as a trainer on the animal movie, "Homeward Bound." I've also supplied many of the animals used as models by Disney animators. My animals have been in a whole raft of television shows, and in magazines and catalogues, commercials produced for companies like Telus and Fido and ICBC, and numerous music videos and CD covers.

At the same time, we've been expanding our offerings in terms of services in order to raise awareness of these animals. We still do presentations in classrooms and at the correctional institute, but now we're also talking to people at trade shows and other public events and venues, like libraries.

Every second summer, Cinemazoo is asked to come and present for the libraries at their summer reading clubs. They get such big crowds coming for these presentations that some of them have had to ask us to do the presentation outside, and they provide a tent for us because their facilities aren't big enough. One library that did this told us they'd had to turn away 150 people the last time they asked us to come, so they had to get a tent this time.

Not too long ago, one of my assistants and I were heading up to a library in Vancouver, and as we got closer to the library, we saw a line coming out of the door and down the block and then around the corner of the block and out of sight. My assistant said, "What's the line-up for? Are they waiting for the library to open or something?" I said, "I'm not sure, but I think that might be for us." Sure enough, that line-up was for us.

I've had people come up to me at trade shows and tell me that they only reason they came was to see me and my animals. I've got adults now telling me that they first saw me when they were five years old and I came to do a birthday party for them. Now they're in their twenties and having kids of their own. They say, "I've still got a picture of you and that snake on my neck on my fridge, you know, from when I was a kid." It feels good.

I've received numerous requests from various media for interviews and appearances. I've been interviewed about wrangling and being an animal agent for television shows like "Vicki Gabereau" and CBC's "the fifth estate." I was interviewed for the twenty-fifth anniversary production of "On the Road Again," and I've been on several episodes of "the Pet Guys," not to mention numerous interviews in magazines worldwide. A few years ago I was even asked to appear on a television show about phobias. Not surprisingly, the phobias had to do with animals like spiders and snakes.

The show itself was part of a series hosted by a psychologist, Dr. Don Dutton, who was on staff at UBC. The doctor would have actors role-play a real issue, and then he'd discuss possible treatments. In this case, the situation involved a couple who wanted to be married, but the guy had 35 snakes as pets and his girlfriend had a serious snake phobia. The psychologist had to come up with a compromise solution.

The first thing I had to do was get the actor who was playing the guy with snakes to be comfortable with snakes. He was actually quite afraid of them. So I had to work with him, plus several of the crew on set who were also afraid. After the show was over, Dr. Dutton came over to talk with me. He said he was impressed with how I'd been able to help those on set conquer their fear and wondered if—since I had the animals and had seemed to help those on set that day—I might be able to help other people with phobias. I don't know if he sent them, but over the next few years, several people with phobias of all manner of animals—frogs, birds, insects, spiders, rats, and of course, snakes—came to see me. They just said they'd been sent from UBC.

It's gratifying to see these things happening and to be getting recognition for what I do, because it's been such a struggle to get this kind of acceptance and interest.

Demand for public performances has led once again to an increase in the number of animals I have, and so once again I've had to expand my space. I'm now renting two buildings here, and I'm thinking of expanding even further. I also have my very own apartment separate from the zoo, but I must confess, it's just next door. It was really time for that to happen if I wanted to have any kind of a love life . . . at least one that didn't involve animals.

Because I could have had Stewie, you know. Good story.

This building used to be a bank, and when I first moved in here, I decided a good place to make my own little home was in this room upstairs that used to be the safe for the bank. It was a pretty big room, about 12 feet by 12 feet. Actually, when I think about it, that was actually kind of ironic—I was living in a safe in a bank because I didn't have any money. Well, that and I always like to live close to the animals. I had it fixed up very nice. I slept on a high captain's bed and there were drawers underneath.

Anyway, one night I'm sleeping and I'm having a very nice dream about a woman. In the dream I feel something licking my ears, and as I slowly come awake I also hear breathing. I'm thinking, "Hey, this is real." But when I open my eyes, staring me in the face is this incredibly cross-eyed possum. It's Stewie—short for Possum Stew.

That possum was lots of fun . . . and really cross-eyed. I mean, most possums are cross-eyed, but Stewie was way out there, so to speak. Stewie had obviously escaped from his cage downstairs and found his way up to where I was. He'd crawled up onto the bed and was licking my ears. I was just too tired to get up and take him back downstairs, so I thought I'd just wait and see what he did. After awhile, Stewie crawled under the blanket and curled up and went to sleep beside me. First time in my life I've ever slept with a possum. Well, that suggests it happened again. It didn't. He kind of smelled, and so did I in the morning.

I would say the main disappointment of this place so far is that it's been hard to get the nature clubs going again. Those clubs were really successful in the Burnaby location, but parents don't want to bring their kids to this neighbourhood, and I've also not been able to find an instructor as good as the one I had in Burnaby. I'm trying to get it going again, though, because I love having the kids come here.

This area of Surrey—known as Whalley—has got its problems, I have to admit. It's known for drugs and prostitution and other kinds of crime. Mostly, though, people are poor, and so a lot of the problems you see go with poverty, like dysfunctional families and other social problems. I could move from here, but moving the zoo is a major undertaking, and also I'm just not ready to give up on Whalley yet. A lot of people won't come into the area because of the reputation, but I actually think there's a lot of potential here. I feel for the street people, too. Some of them have had pretty hard lives. Some might have chosen the paths they've taken, but most haven't, and my heart goes out to them. No right-thinking person chooses to live on the street strung out on crack. Maybe because of my time living on Vancouver's Downtown Eastside, I'm able to identify with them a bit more than most.

Anyway, my way of dealing with it is to try to change it. First thing I did was join the Whalley Business Improvement Association. Then I got to know the street people as well as the business and service folks. Now I'm co-chairperson for an organization called Acorn that acts on behalf of the residents and businesses in the area to convince the government that change is needed. And things are starting to change, like, there are getting to be fewer pawnshops and sex shops; things like that.

Through Acorn and through the Business Improvement Association, I've also become familiar with the police and fire personnel in the area. It's funny: when the fire department comes for the yearly inspection of Cinemazoo, they bring their families. I'm not sure they're seeing half the stuff that might be wrong with the building because they're so busy looking at the animals, like, "Oh, what's that? Is that an alligator?"

Everyone I've talked to—and I go to a lot of public meetings addressing improvement in this area—seems to appreciate that I care, including the street people. One time I had a couple of bicycles stolen from the back of my place that belonged to my employees, so I went to the street people and I said, "Look,

someone swiped a couple of bikes from me. What can you do?"
Within a few days, we had the bikes back.

The street people respect me because I treat them decently. I
treat them like humans. I don't come out throwing things at them
and yelling and screaming things like: "Get off my property you
useless bag of whatever." You know, I've seen some of the business owners do that. I just talk with them. Sometimes we even
talk about alternate choices. I don't know how they got there, so
I'm not going to judge them. I explain to them that I've got kids
coming around the place, and I say, "If you had kids would you
want them to see this?" They say, "No problem. We'll move."
They're very cooperative if you talk to them like they're humans.
I've been here six years now, and the worst thing that's ever
happened to me is having those two bikes stolen, and I got them
back.

Maybe it wasn't the best move I could have made, but I don't
regret it. I never regret decisions I've made because they have,
as my grandfather promised, always been good learning experiences. And frequently led to other, better experiences, like in this
case, becoming involved in the politics of community change,
something I might never have experienced otherwise. And even
if I haven't been able to get the nature clubs going, I've moved
ahead with something that I've wanted to do for ages: I've opened
up a career school for people who want to work with animals.

This desire comes from my own experience once it became
clear that I couldn't become a vet, the experience of having
nowhere else to go that might help me learn a skill that would lead
to a career where I could work with animals and still make money.
There just isn't much out there in terms of training for things like
becoming an animal trainer, or a wrangler, or even how to run a
dog daycare in a thoughtful and responsible way. I've done so
many of these things now, and I'm at a place in my life where I
want to start passing some of it on. Students who come here are
able to learn wildlife and pet photography, plus dog grooming
and care for animals in general. Recently I've brought in a woman
who specializes in massage therapy for animals. I've even found a
vet who said he'd be more than willing to come in and talk about
the care and maintenance of exotic animals from a veterinarian's
point of view.

One of the areas of great interest for students is zoo-keeping,
and I've been fortunate enough to obtain a marvellous manual

on training people to become zookeepers. The manual was co-authored by a man who—as it happens—was the godfather of the girl who took over the dog daycare at the Burnaby location. Cor Jansen was a famous zoologist and zookeeper: He'd been the director of the zoo in Honolulu, and had once been in charge of the Assiniboine Park Zoo in Manitoba. The manual is a veritable goldmine of information, and he charged me only a few thousand dollars for it; far less than was paid for it by places like the San Diego and Berlin zoos.

They start by learning a little bit about all kinds of different career choices, and then as they become more aware of what's out there and what interests them, their study becomes more focused. The school has been going for a few years now. We're still working out some of the details, but we're getting close to having something quite comprehensive to offer. We've already had people come from as far away as Sweden, Germany, Australia, and England.

I'm still disappointed that I couldn't be a vet, but in the end, I think I've gained a much broader experience with animals than I would have if I'd focused on just that one profession. In fact, I had many vets tell me that they make good money doing what they're doing, but the reality of practice is not quite as exciting as they had envisioned while they were still in school.

So all in all, I took the right route. I've worked with such a variety of animals—and, for that matter, I've assisted many vets—and although I sometimes call in a vet for a sick animal, there are many times I've had to do my own vet work. If there's a broken wing, for instance, I fix it myself. If I'm not already familiar with the issue at hand, I'll usually read up on it before calling the vet. For instance, today I noticed wetness at the dock of the tails on my sugar gliders. Sugar gliders are small gliding possums that originally come from Australia or New Guinea's part of the world. Their tails shouldn't be wet, but these are, so it's a symptom of something and it needs to be addressed. I need to go to my library and delve into my research books to see if I can find out anything there. If I can't, then I'll bring in a vet.

These things though—the school, the nature clubs, all the things I'm doing that help raise awareness of these animals—these are my main focus now. This is where I want to be putting my effort and time. But these things are not big money-makers, and it's costly to keep the animals. I feed my animals the best quality organic fresh fruit and vegetables and they get only fresh meat and fish. I go through 1000 crickets a week, and I raise my own rats and mice to ensure there's a steady supply of fresh food for the carnivores. I have staff as well, who must be paid—three full-time workers, plus seven who are a mix of part-time and volunteer.

My ultimate goal is to build a state-of-the-art animal ecology centre. I think maybe that might be the last door.

28 The Final Door?

I've been thinking about this ecology centre for a long time—years and years and years. I've visited various serpentariums and zoos, aviaries and entomology displays. I've taken the best ideas out of all they have to offer, and I now have this centre all planned out. It will be a refuge for reptiles, insects, birds, and other exotic animals. But it won't just be a zoo: it will be an educational centre where people can come to learn about these animals. It will be a research facility and a place for nature clubs and a career school. It will be a place where a family can bring their children and talk about the animals, where the kids can see that they can join a club to learn more, and where they can choose to attend career school when they graduate from high school.

Some species of exotic animals are endangered, so one of the goals for the centre would be to replenish diminishing stocks. Beyond the fact that they're fascinating animals, they're necessary to our survival—these guys vanish first when our environment is under threat. They're the canaries in the coal mine.

I think we're also looking at a time not that far away when these kinds of exotic animals will be less and less available to the film world because of growing protests from animal activists, and from simply having less of them around because some species may become extinct. I'd like to create a studio on site where the animals can be photographed or filmed in a safe and supportive environment.

Finally, I'd like to create a separate facility located nearby that provides a safe and comfortable holding place for animals working in media. So for instance, the guy I mentioned earlier who brought his chimpanzees here in his self-contained truck would have a better place to house his animals while they're here for filming. The owners would have the benefit of knowing that if the animals needed special care, there would be on-site veterinarians and assistant trainers. The animals would be fed top-quality food and regularly stimulated. There would be night security so that this guy and his wife could rest comfortably in a hotel if they chose.

I truly believe there is a need for what I've got in mind. Places like the Vancouver Aquarium house the marine and aquatic animals, larger zoos carry the bigger animals like the giraffes, rhinos, hippos and zebras. I want to house the in-between animals. I hope it will be my legacy, my way of giving back to the animals, because everything worthwhile I've done in life has been because of them.

I love what I do. It's not the money (thank goodness, or I'd be in a bad way). It's the challenge, and the gratification I get from working with these animals and making their lives in captivity as good as they can be. And it's the thought that maybe I'll get an opportunity to take it all a step further with the centre and make a positive difference for animals and people in the future. That's what drives me. That's what keeps me going.

Not that I wouldn't like a bit of financial security. Yes, please! Even without the centre, the zoo needs more full-time staff, and I really do need to move the birds. The parrots, especially, need an aviary—a place where they can fly free. And after many years of bachelorhood, I'm in a committed relationship now with someone I really love and who complements and supports what I do. Sandy deserves a nicer home than my little place behind the zoo, so a move to a real home is in our plans for the near future.

My family has never understood my living arrangements. For that matter, I've always felt a bit of an oddball in our family, but recently my aunt told me that the family was proud of me. She said, "You've stuck it out all these years and kept your belief in what you're doing. Good for you. We all support you, Gary." It was a very important seal of approval for me.

You know, I don't personally feel like I'm a success yet, but I do feel I've made a name for myself and the zoo, and I think there's more to come. I've sure gone through a lot of doors—from first learning about and then collecting insects, to the training I took to become a horse guard, to becoming a horse trainer, to rounding up animals for the Toronto zoo, even to becoming a fashion photographer. It's all contributed to where I am today.

Taking the route I've taken has been hard. I've had a lot of struggles over the years I've had Cinemazoo, but I always knew it was the right door. From the time I first said the name, "Cinem-azoo," I knew this was what I had to do and that it was going to lead me to my ultimate goal. My grandfather was right: When one door closes, another one opens. I'm always looking for the open door.

I think the biggest compliment my mother ever gave me was just before she died and I was with her in the hospital. She said, "You know, Gary, if your grandfather is looking down on your life, he must be proud of you, because you've not only gone through the doors he talked about, but you've gone through more than he did. He's proud of you, and I am too." That was a huge thing for her to say to me, because my mom had a lot of ups and downs about my career choices, and she wasn't an affectionate person, so it really meant a lot. I put my arms around her and gave her a hug. That was ten years ago. It was the last time I saw her.

One last story, okay?

My mom died soon after that last visit with her, and I went back to Toronto for the funeral. She and my dad had moved back to Toronto a few years before. Anyway, my sister had taken care of all the funeral arrangements, and those included having an open casket for three days, during which time (as her son) I had to be present at the funeral home to receive guests. Well, lots of people came to pay their final respects to Mom, but there were also many times when nothing was happening, and much as I loved my mom, I got bored just sitting there looking at her. So I would wander around.

Now, this was a big funeral home. There were about nine other chambers where there were other open caskets. I would peek in and sometimes talk to other families who were there. Frequently, though, the chamber would be empty, and in those cases I'd look in at the person and try to imagine what they were like and what kind of life they'd led and so on.

I was standing beside this one casket holding an old guy who'd never had a visitor; not one soul had come to see him. He had a strong image that kind of reminded me of my grandfather. As I was looking at him and thinking about things, I took out a package of Certs and popped one in my mouth. Then I thought, "I wonder if he wants one?" So I took a Certs out and I tried putting it in his mouth. I couldn't put it in and I didn't want to force it, so I just put it in his breast pocket. My sister walked in just then and she said, "Gary, what are you doing?"

I said, "I'm giving him Certs."

"Are you crazy? What are you doing that for?"

"Well, you don't know who he's going to meet wherever he's going. At least he'll have nice breath." She was shaking her head in disbelief. I said, "You know, there's another point. What if they have to exhume the body? You know instead of opening up a casket and getting this awful smell, it would be nice to get a whiff of Certs."

She said, "You're nuts."

So then I got the idea. Whenever a chamber was empty, I'd walk in and put Certs in the casket with them. I went through maybe ten Certs that way because one of the chambers had a changeover. Some might think this was a bit weird, but I thought it was kind of cool. I know I'm taking a package of Certs with me when I go. Fruit-flavoured.

But I've got a lot of work to do before that happens.

I mean, there will come a time when I won't be physically able to keep up this pace, but I hope that by that time I'll have created this fantastic facility. I hope I'll still be a part of it, too, in whatever capacity. I have this image of the facility management talking to a newcomer in the business and pointing out the window at this old guy working in the garden, and they're saying, "Hey, there's the guy who started it."

For me, that's the final door. That's how I want to leave this world, knowing that I've opened that door for everybody else. In the meantime, though, I've got lots of adventures to experience, lots of things to learn. That's what I love about animals—you never stop learning, you never stop meeting people, you never stop having adventures, and you never run out of doors.

Epilogue

Four years have passed since this story was first written. Gary continues to rescue animals and continues his educational outreach to audiences throughout British Columbia's Lower Mainland. He's no longer with Sandy, but they parted amicably and remain friends.

Notably, in the past year, Gary fought the battle of his life trying to save his animals in the face of a new provincial government regulation banning the ownership of many of the animals he rescued and cared for over the years. On the face of it, it's a law that Gary agrees with, but it's a law that does not make a distinction between the average animal owner and someone like Gary, who has devoted most of his life to understanding and working with animals and ensuring their survival. On top of this, another provincial government regulation has made it almost impossible for him to continue his educational outreach.

Gary has made several attempts to bring about a situation in which he can keep the animals he's had for years. As mentioned earlier, that story is documented and available online as a web series, "Saving Cinemazoo".

www.savingcinemazoo.com

In December 2009, when Gary was facing bankruptcy and eviction, a financial expert R. Robert Allan, volunteered his assistance and coached Gary through his bankruptcy, while handling the financial affairs of the business and society. "We now affectionately call him 'the money dude'," says Gary. At the time of writing, Gary was starting over again, revamping Cinemazoo and going through yet another door.

Gary Oliver's relationship with animals began when he was seven. Soon he began trading bug specimens with like-minded souls around the world, which he followed by volunteering at the ROM (the Royal Ontario Museum).

From bugs, his passion for animals expanded and working with animals became his lifelong goal. In his early twenties, he became a cavalry trooper in the Governor General's Horse Guards.

In 1973, he moved west and graduated in Fine Arts from Capilano College in North Vancouver. Gary's opportunistic founding of the Pacific Artists Studios offered a communal space for the up and coming. All told, 314 artists got their start in those 30 studios set in the heart of downtown Vancouver.

Fashion photography and Maynard—a star feline performer— led him to open Cinemazoo, Canada's first animal agency. Through Cinemazoo, Gary has wrangled elephants, llamas, snakes and frogs, as well as dogs and cats for countless films, television commercials and corporate events.

What began as an agency soon became a refuge for animals and Cinemazoo became home to countless abandoned exotic animals. In 2007, he founded the Urban Safari Rescue Society as a non-profit rescue organization. (www.urbansafarirescue.ca)

Thousands of schools, public institutions, corporations and non-profit organizations have benefitted from his educational talks and hands-on demonstrations. His mission is to educate the public about the conservation and sustainability of wildlife. As adults, it is our responsibility to teach our children that they *can* make a difference. Kids need nature. Nature needs kids.

Wendy Bancroft is an award-winning writer and documentary film producer. As a television current affairs journalist—primarily with the Canadian Broadcasting Corporation, hosting their regional current affairs program, the *Pacific Report*—her stories reflect an interest in the human condition and how people face the challenges in their lives.

After leaving the CBC, Wendy earned her masters degree in political science from the University of British Columbia, and then became a senior researcher with two national research organizations. Recently, she has returned to making films with her own company, "It's About Us Productions." Many of her films focus on work and what it means to those who do it. As her mother always said (and, according to Wendy, she did say it a lot): "If a job's worth doing, it's worth doing well." Wendy's latest work isthe production of the web series *Saving Cinemazoo*.

Index

To learn more about Gary and Cinemazoo, please visit:
www.cinemazoo.com
www.savingcinemazoo.com
www.urbansafarirescue.ca